OBEDIENCE

OBEDIENCE

The One Thing God Wants Most

DOUG POOLE

XULON PRESS

Xulon Press
2301 Lucien Way #415
Maitland, FL 32751
407.339.4217
www.xulonpress.com

Printed in the United States of America

Paperback ISBN-13: 978-1-66283-736-4
Hard Cover ISBN-13: 978-1-66283-737-1
Ebook ISBN-13: 978-1-66283-738-8

Other Books by Doug Poole

Coming Before the Lord
(2019)

Book trailer:
https://www.christianfaithpublishing.com/
books/?book=coming-before-the-lord

Remember the Word
(2020)

Stages of Life
(2021)

www.DougPoole.net

www.amazon.com/books/doug-poole

Table of Contents

The Impression

I am told by those who write for a living that it is good to start by out-lining what the book is to include. My education did not include that bit of knowledge, but I do like the idea. It would be wise to know what you want to communicate and plan to convey best all intended to complete your manuscript.

So far, the problem I have in following this format is the way I receive the unction of information which is a prompting from the Lord. Since my memory is limited, I panic and write as fast as possible to get the information down on paper. If I did depend on memory, much would be lost, and I would not completely convey the message being impressed on me.

Knowing this, I've learned that I really can't accomplish anything of worth without the Lord. John 15:5 tells me I can do nothing without Him. What does that mean? It means that to achieve any godly fruit, I must stay connected with the source. Jesus is the source. And it's easy to see as I got into working for Him in writing, my reliance was sub-stantially greater than I first realized — especially to write this book.

My impression from the Lord came as I sat on the couch and looked at my niece's photo. After thinking of all her natural abilities and talents, I was amazed by her potential. I didn't have hardly any of her qualities, making our differences significant. It's not that I'm of less value to the Lord, but it does mean she has a much greater natural ability to write a book than I do.

When I laid the picture down immediately, the Lord started to pour in what He wanted me to write. It was a whole new thought, and I had no doubt it was from Him. As I began writing it down, I was surprised at the title and the chapter titles that came pouring into my mind. This event all took place in about ten minutes, and then it stopped. I sat in amazement because I had a much different idea in mind about what my next book would be titled.

I was prayerful about which book to start first, and He reminded me this was coming from Him with urgency, so it had precedence over any other thought I might have had before. Following His leading would require me to follow what this book is about and respond in obedience. Well, that was interesting to me and opened up my understanding to put into practice what He was prompting me immediately.

It is always interesting how the Lord prompts each believer. That includes similarities but also is uniquely different for each person. Some folks have dreams, some have significantly different experiences, and some relay that the Lord spoke to them. My promptings from the Lord are precise and usually catch me by surprise. I have been awakened from sleep with a particular idea to write down and an idea that is very precise, fast, direct, and to the point.

I always tell everyone I'm a little stubborn, and it requires determined insistence to get me moving in the right direction. I compare myself to the donkey the prophet Balaam was riding in Numbers chapter 22. Since the prophet was not minding the Lord, He used a donkey speaking to him to convey His message.

I believe that I have a hard time hearing from the Lord because I'm a little like the prophet Balaam and am stubborn as a donkey. I have my idea of which way to go in life, and the Lord needs to be very direct with me to get my attention. Well, learning to write about what the Lord prompts me has been very interesting as I look back on His promptings and guidance.

This writing will be my fourth book for the Lord, and I'm getting better at hearing His voice and following His leading. Listening is a choice, just like obedience. My hearing is improving, and my Obedience to follow Him is getting easier the older I get. Maybe one day, He will discuss all the mercy he sent my way to get me through life. I realize my character needs to change, and my learning to listen more intently could be significantly improved.

Life with the Lord is extraordinary and receiving promptings from Him is very exciting to me. I want to live a long time, so I can continue to follow His leading and get better at what He wants me to do. If writing is my direction, I want to be pleasing to Him and operate in the supernatural rather than trudge along only in the natural realm.

I never thought I could be used this way in a million years, and I get more confident all the time because I'm learning new things all along the way. Experiencing God is a beautiful thing, and I truly believe He wants to be in a relationship with each believer in a personal way. This theme of fellowship is woven throughout the Bible and is as real today as it was thousands of years ago.

It's fun to be a part of what God is doing on the earth today and knowing He has invited all believers to work for Him as He prepares His Bride, the Church, for a journey home to our designated place in Heaven. I so look forward to that meeting when His Church is called home, and I will get to spend Eternity with the LORD!

Introduction

The Bible has remained a tremendous source of information referenced throughout this book. Obtaining knowledge backed up by Scriptures to what the Lord impresses on me is quite encouraging. My learning about Him from both the Old and New Testaments is very fulfilling. It has been a surge of wisdom only God can provide and much needed to open my understanding.

The subjects I once knew very little about have become alive as the Holy Spirit leads me into God's Word. The enlightenment to my understanding and the wisdom I learn increases my faith to move forward, knowing that the Lord is building character within and wisdom that is above and beyond the worldly knowledge I've accumulated.

This book will provide scriptural references to many situations we all commonly experience in life. Thinking we are alone in this dark world is not a correct perspective. God's Word is God's knowledge in print that, when applied, creates wisdom for our experiencing. It comes alive to provide the proper guidance and correct direction needed to overcome natural occurrences, circumstances, and feelings and emotions we encounter.

We all tend to be led by our emotions and feelings rather than being led by the Word of God. This tendency is prevalent with each of us. Following the Truth of God's Word means we have to act in faith and move in the instructed direction prescribed without preference for our natural feelings and emotions.

Acting in faith is very difficult, at first, even scary, and sometimes it seems ridiculous. Choosing to go in a direction that is not natural or doesn't seem logical can be frightening. Once you begin to practice operating in the spiritual mode, it does gradually becomes more effortless. As we move in faith and proceed under His guidance, we learn that our circumstances will begin to change as well as our character and trust in Him.

The Bible is full of stories where moving in faith rather than by our natural responses has brought great confidence in God into existence. It has allowed the Lord to show Himself directly, leading the complete procession forward and accomplishing precisely what the Word of God is teaching us.

As you read this book and the Bible-inspired Truth it offers, I believe you will understand that the Bible is alive and more than ready to instruct us in solutions we can't even imagine on our own. I can't give you all the reasons it is so perfect for humankind, but I can tell you it works perfectly, and I'm a living witness to its changing effects in my own life.

Obedience is a critical area that we humans tend to shy away from because we have a wrong connotation. Because the Lord gave us all the freedom to choose for ourselves, we tend to lean away from Him and rely on our understanding instead. Keeping our distance from all it offers reveals that we choose to do things our way and depend on our knowledge rather than His.

Your understanding of obedience can be altered when you start understanding its purpose and what God promises as you follow His instructions and learn His wisdom. His Word will change many things about your thinking, and it will prove to be reliable when fully applied.

This learning and understanding will be contrary to your natural thinking, so be aware and don't be surprised when you put it into action. The results will bring prosperity and success. It won't necessarily be immediate, but it will prevail if you allow God to complete His work in His time frame. The waiting can sometimes bring anxiety, but the wait will build character in you and build your trust in His instructions if you will but let it play out and believe — in faith.

Chapter 1

Why so Many Problems?

Living our lives consist of many problems that are not avoidable. That is the way life presents itself, and no one is immune from experiencing them. If you find your life without problems, I assure you — you're already dead. There's no need to check your pulse — your dead.

As a child, one of my first thoughts regarding accepting the Lord was now there wouldn't be any more problems. I moved forward in believing that lie and found out shortly there was no truth in it. How did I find out? Nothing changed. All remained just the same. I did get a little excited that I was now saved and going to heaven, but that didn't help me right at that moment.

Relying on my childhood knowledge set me back a bit, but I was only six without a long history or experience to keep me from getting over the apparent reality. I knew I felt better inside, which carried me over and taught me my first truth about life and what might be expected in my future. My childhood thinking had failed me, and I just needed to get over it.

It didn't take long to see skepticism that accompanied my new standing with the Lord, and I figured I now had more problems than before. It wasn't terrible or anything, but my telling others I was saved certainly didn't bring the house down in applause.

As I grew in age, knowledge about the Bible, my wanting to put it into practice just didn't happen. I remained with my natural thinking based on life as I saw it and on what I witnessed with my family around me. Applying scriptural principles didn't come into view, nor did I understand it should. I just knew I was saved, and eternity with the Lord awaited me when my life ended.

Being young then meant you were to be still, unopinionated, quiet when company came to visit, mind your parent's rules, and avoid mischief. I certainly was not silent, loved to visit with people, was pretty good at minding my parents, and was always curious about all around me. I was very active (not still), very opinionated because I had gathered a lot of information from listening to other adults. I loved to see how 'things' worked, so taking objects apart was of great interest to me.

Since trouble usually occurred during assembly, I would take apart something, like an old clock, and carefully lay the pieces down in a designated sequence of removal to see how each piece functioned with the others and then reassemble. Once I was satisfied and understood its function or thought I did, I could usually fix one in the future if it ever stopped working.

From all of this, I learned to reassemble it quickly and put it back together, set the time, check the alarm, and move on to the next item of interest. Oh yes, and never tell anyone what I did. Why? Because I was so young, I considered this as a covert operation and not dishonestly.

From believing this Bible statement in Psalms, I'm not altogether at fault for being so curious. Since I believe the Lord intricately weaves us together in our mother's womb and creates us precisely the way we are (Psalm 119:15), I have an excuse. My excuse is that the Lord made me this way, and I can't help it. It can be considered inquisitive anyway, and that sounds much better from where I sit.

As a child, I enjoyed going to the hardware store in town and looking at each item hanging or laying on a shelf and trying to determine how it worked. Disassembly was usually avoided, but I liked studying each item and seeing what it did and how it was designed, and for what purpose. Today, I still enjoy looking through stuff, machinery, tools, mechanical devices, specific designs, etc. I can get excited when I remember a tool or design that I saw that can be used somewhere else with a completely different purpose.

I'm easily entertained, and with a bit of humor and a fantastic, imaginative process, many possibilities are always present. My mind continually provides me with entertainment in almost every situation. I find humor in nearly everything, which has been both fun and a few times embarrassing. It depends on what crowd you're with that day that will give you their feedback. Funny comes in many colors, and recipients vary greatly as well.

Our natural mind and thinking make it difficult to wait on the Lord and listen when praying rather than talking the whole time. If you want to know what is on the Lord's heart — you have to shut up and listen. Need I say this is not my strong suit. I don't think many folks like waiting on the Lord, but it does eventually come with practice, and for me, lots of it. I am getting better all the time.

As a result of moving at sonic speed, humankind tends to bypass waiting on God and then wonder why so many problems exist in their life. I also believe our good ideas are gathered from a limited human thinking stockpile based on human experiences, advice from others, and accumulated knowledge that logically seems correct.

God's stockpile consists of His wisdom and understanding of how 'things' really operate because He is the Creator and has assembled everything in existence and fully connects each working piece and how it functions (read Job chapter 38). His knowing this places Him in full knowledge of how life works — every detail.

The Bible provides written confirmation of His wisdom and knowledge and provides realistic understanding put into words that teach us how to navigate our lives. Should we follow His instructions, our problems will be met with a surprising victory in overcoming our environment and circumstances with better results and minimizing repeated difficulties in our future.

Worldly knowledge is always available, but it usually does not equip us with complete results that eliminate the problem. Sometimes worldly understanding only deals with a symptom of the problem and does not eliminate the root cause. If I understand Scripture and its repeated message, I would formulate that we comprehend in logical partial thinking, and God understands in the fullness of wisdom.

So what's the problem? We don't understand enough of our environment to be very effective in resolving the issues on our own, and we need God's help to overcome. The whole idea of God's Word, Jesus our Savior, and the Holy Spirit are to enable us with His power and wisdom to plow through life and benefit from His many provisions. Our life on earth is not a long time. It passes much quicker than you may think. And, only one passage through is allowed — no repeats.

We all struggle in life, so the sooner we start applying God's principles and learning His ways, the better we navigate this vessel in which we live. Applying His principles is so much more effective than ours. And, the sooner we start utilizing His wisdom, the greater and quicker we reap the benefits. His guidance provides us with much greater joy and peace during our journey. That is just the way things are!

Want to eliminate many problems in your life? Stop trying to figure everything out on your own. Start gathering godly wisdom from the Bible and apply its principles in your life. Do you realize that using our natural thinking in life only deals with a portion of what's out there? Along with the natural world in which we live, there is also a spiritual realm that surrounds us. The natural abilities we possess cannot operate against anything in the spiritual world.

Our inability in the natural and the lack of knowledge or power to fully deal with our surroundings positions us in a very venerable predicament. Since the spiritual world is all around us and the natural, don't you think our effectiveness will be limited at best? We can't see or protect ourselves against evil spiritual forces, so what are we supposed to do?

The answer is quite simple. Decide to follow after the Creator's path of instructions and reap the rewards! This decision to choose a better way, His way, will place you on a path of fewer problems. Not choosing to follow after Him keeps us powerless, venerable, weak, unknowing, limited, and certainly in the dark when understanding what is necessary and required.

Knowing a better way exists should encourage your hope for a better future and raise your curiosity to know what more there is. Jesus didn't come and visit us on earth to start a mystery story about some prophet that may or may not exist and begin a religion of rules and regulations. He came for a reason, and we can be the heirs of that purpose. We see in Revelation 5 that the Lamb of God, Jesus, came to purchase the human race by the shedding of His blood for our redemption.

Jesus Ransoms People For God

If your life is left to chance, it can be summed up with a bleak future and problems that will never change much or benefit your growth in becoming a better person (Christlike). Worldly knowledge will provide you with limited success and keep you on the same path with the assurance that eternal damnation will undoubtedly follow. Is that your idea of an exciting existence and future? When you get my age, a rocker awaits you at the location of your life's end resulting in no hope for the future. This is not the location or condition where I want to end up.

There is good reason to believe the Lord allows problems to get our attention. If everything went smoothly, there would be no need for God or anything He offers. Life would be a breeze, and we would never be motivated to do much of anything in seeking after His help.

The Bible has threaded throughout its many situations that required God's help to resolve problems. Most of the solutions were not what we would imagine. They were solutions only God could perform — not man.

Take, for example, the problem of hunger and thirst. This physical need can be quenched with food and water. These areas fall into the natural realm and can be found with our abilities to gather what we require to exist and function normally. Some parts of the world have greater struggles to obtain these necessities, but they are necessary to meet our physical requirements for nourishment to our body. No spiritual help is needed.

Weather is another element of our natural world. It provides many necessities required to produce conditions needed to grow food for survival and can also create conditions that bring difficulty and problems we would rather avoid. No spiritual assistance is required here either for us to experience.

Now, what about problems in the area of the spiritual realm? Maybe you've encountered nagging thoughts that you're worthless, stupid, unworthy of living, or have negative thoughts and feelings about yourself. Ever wonder where these ideas come from? Well, you should. They have a source.

Negative thoughts that seem to be whispered into your mind come from the devil. His goal is to terminate your life before you find out that Jesus came to save your soul from eternal damnation. The devil of our spiritual world is Satan, and he is seeking, continually, to steal, kill, and destroy everyone (John 10:10).

This spiritual realm exists all around us living on the earth today. It is not something that exists without the Lord's knowledge. He has allowed it, and we who are living have to deal with its presence. Since God is aware, He has provided a spiritual protection plan that offers weapons to ward off the enemy and overcome with His tools of weaponry, as explained in Ephesians chapter 6 in the New Testament.

The Bible is clear regarding this spiritual enemy and instructions on how to deal with this evil force. This spiritual enemy is not something spooky to scare anyone, but it shows us who our enemy is and how to deal with it successfully.

As stated earlier, the devil has a specific purpose while his spiritual kingdom remains in operation. Satan is said in Scripture to be roaming around seeking someone he can mess with to carry out his mission. Look at the following verses and see how this came into being and what we have to deal with:

1 Peter 5:8
"Be sober, be vigilant; because your adversary the devil walks about like a roaring lion, seeking whom he may devour."

2 Peter 2:4-6
"For if God did not spare the angels who sinned, but cast them down to hell and delivered them into chains of darkness, to be reserved for judgment; and did not spare the ancient world, but saved Noah, one of eight people, a preacher of righteousness, bringing in the flood on the world of the ungodly; and turning the cities of Sodom and Gomorrah into ashes, condemned them to destruction, making them an example to those who afterward would live ungodly."

The purpose of evil and how we deal with its presence become apparent as we read Scripture. And, we learn how to counteract against this evil spiritual realm that accompanies us throughout life. Don't ask me all the reasons why evil exists because I don't have an answer. I just believe the Bible and know evil is present.

John 10:10
"The thief's (Satan's) purpose is to steal and kill and destroy. My purpose (Jesus) is to give them a rich and satisfying life."

We are up against the forces of evil, according to John chapter 10:10. Looking at life from God's perspective, we see from the following verse

7

in Ephesians, which gives us a description of Satan's existence and what we are dealing with:

Ephesians 6:12
"For we are not fighting against flesh-and-blood enemies, but against evil rulers and authorities of the unseen world, against mighty powers in this dark world, and against evil spirits in the heavenly places."

Make no mistake and brush off the presence of a spiritual realm in which we all live. We are born into this physical world and subject to all its environment. We are subject to its natural laws that affect us all and the spiritual realm in the earth and its existence and effects. During our existence here, we must function in this environment to live out our lives. It's just the way things are living on earth, whether we believe it or not.

Our existence here on earth is for whatever duration God has granted to each person. He is well aware of our conditions and has provided a means to maneuver through with His help and guidance. The Bible offers just what we require to live life to the fullest. The biblical approach may seem odd, but its principles and application will operate so well today that you will be amazed!

Now the next thought needs to be directed at what do you believe? Are you receptive to what God says, or do you discount it as old rubbish and of no use to you? If I were you, I would search for what God has offered and seek it out for myself. Logical thinking and worldly wisdom directly oppose God's Word and are scripturally described as strongholds of wrong thinking (2 Corinthians 10:4).

Hence, we have a choice to either utilize His provisions or deny them. He created us to choose for ourselves how we want to live a full and meaningful life. There are no have to's in living out our natural existence. We can pass through life however we decide to move along.

God does provide the option to call upon Him for help in dealing with any conditions. His provisions equip us to maneuver through life on a very different plane that will surpass what our natural abilities and thinking can offer.

The biblical approach is beyond our realm of understanding and seems rather strange if we judge its completeness from our original, born into this world condition as a human being. It will sound a little odd, but when practiced, you will find it is precisely how things exist in this world in which we function.

These are factual points of most significant interest from the Bible that require our utmost attention should we desire to indulge in becoming a believer and overcomer in the Lord. These facts are not visible or obtainable without the Lord's help and are identified throughout all of Scripture.

See How Scripture Declares our Awareness to our Environment without His Help

John 12:40
*"The Lord has blinded (**typhloo**) their eyes and hardened their hearts—so that their eyes cannot see, and their hearts cannot understand, and they cannot turn to me and have me heal them."*

This Scripture tells me we are spiritually blind without the Lord in our lives. We may see in the natural, but viewing anything other than physical objects is not possible. It appears that only the Lord can bring us spiritual sight, bring understanding to our hearts, and healing; we need to be among the spiritually active. Otherwise, we cannot function successfully in the world.

Let me give you an example of our ability to obtain this needed information as found written in the Bible from the God of Creation, providing it for our understanding. Read the following:

2 Corinthians 4:4
*"Satan, who is the god of this world, has blinded (**typhlos**) the minds of those who don't believe. They are unable to see the glorious light of the*

Good News. They don't understand this message about the glory of Christ, who is the exact likeness of God."

From the above Scripture, you can see that Satan wants to keep us spiritually blind. You can still see with your natural eyesight but remain blind spiritually. We are born into the world this way. So, we are spiritually blind until God removes our blindness when we become a believer. Until we accept Jesus, we will remain blind spiritually.

Only the Lord can bring spiritual eyesight to the spiritually blind. Scripture confirms both situations, about physical and spiritual blindness, and gives us examples of healing for both.

Luke 6:39
*"Then Jesus gave the following illustration: Can one blind (**typhlos**) person lead another? Won't they both fall into a ditch?"*

Thinking you can see spiritually is how the Pharisees viewed life because they depended on their knowledge and understanding to see spiritually. Jesus let them know they were blind spiritually, and their leadership, knowledge of Scripture would neither save them nor give them spiritual vision.

The wisdom humanity accumulates in the natural does not provide sufficient knowledge as God's wisdom does. Because of that, the Pharisees were not seeing what the Lord could make available. Their pride and determination to see things from their perspective only caused them to remain lost and unable to see past themselves.

We can only determine the best solution with spiritual vision — not through our natural logic, physical eyesight, and limited knowledge. We are limited due to our restricted sight and desperately need the veil to be lifted to view life through the eyes of God.

We can certainly see that Scriptures provide a clear picture of our condition and what we view as authentic and relevant in our worldly environment. This scriptural evaluation gives way to understand our visual limitations better. It brings to light our actual condition and lets us see how limited we are without Him. God provided the way to 'see' past ourselves and not remain blind and helpless. The natural realm alone cannot provide us with the eyesight needed to meet the future and understand beyond ourselves.

This healing is a gift the Lord offers to each believer, and it requires an open mind and <u>spiritual vision</u> to receive the things of God. Living has many challenges that occur during our lifetime. We must remain open to the Holy Spirit of God for His guidance to ever expect to overcome all the obstacles that are waiting in our future. This is a reality for everyone — no exceptions.

Believers aren't exempt from life's many challenges. Still, we have the opportunity to call upon the Lord to help us better understand how to maneuver and apply His principles and come out on the other side in much better condition. Utilizing His guidance and wisdom from the Scriptures allows us the opportunity to have an inside edge over the nonbeliever.

As you can imagine, a blind man can adapt to no physical eyesight, but being spiritually blind will not provide any alternative to seeing spiritually. Compare a spiritually blind person headed toward his future to a car moving down the road without a driver. As you would guess, staying on a designated roadway would only be temporary and destined for a fatal conclusion.

I'm sure with physical blindness, you could learn through trial and error how to sense the sound of pavement under your tires, but that wouldn't provide any security in reaching your destination without extreme problems. I'm confident you would quickly decide a better way to travel than driving a car was absolutely necessary.

In like manner with spiritual blindness, you find yourself lost and without direction. Not being able to see spiritually provides no vision of what lies ahead or the ability to deal with it. Our lack of sensitivity to the spiritual realm leaves us totally helpless.

Matthew 13:17

"I tell you the truth, many prophets and righteous people longed to see what you see (physical eyesight), but they didn't see it. And they longed to hear what you hear, but they didn't hear it."

In Matthew, we learn that Christ brought with Him the hopes of many believer's that wanted to see and hear Him for themselves. During the stay of Jesus on earth, the disciples and the people witnessed His very presence. All that God had prophesied about in the Old Testament. It was a fulfillment of Scriptures right in their presents. The completion of Scriptures gives evidence that Jesus was the Christ sent by God among humankind to bring salvation to the whole world.

To search for a deeper meaning in Scripture and decipher God's Word more clearly is to look back at the original language. When that is done, greater meaning can be revealed from God's Word than first appears. Why is this? Because translating each word into English sometimes does not bring with it the full intent or whole meaning of a word in its complete application to what's being said.

Let's look at the following Scripture and do a background check to see if there is more meaning than we see when translated into English. This process illuminates Scripture and broadens our understanding, and brings added meaning to God's Word.

John 9:39

*"Then Jesus told him, 'I entered this world to render judgment—to give sight to the blind (**blepo**) and to show those who think they see that they are blind (**typhlos**).'"*

Viewing the original text reveals that there are two different meanings for the word blind. The original meaning for each word blind must be applied to grasp the direct application and see the whole meaning, which is not revealed when translated to English.

The first word for blind used in this Scripture, from John chapter 9, verse 39, is spelled **blepo**. The spelling of the second word translated blind is **typhlos**. Each word blind has its specific meaning, and when viewed in light of the original text, we can better understand what Jesus is saying.

Now, let us determine the meaning of blind from each spelling from the original language and see how the translation appears under the magnifying glass:

- **Our Natural Eyesight**: The word **blepo** carries with it the meaning of using the physical eyesight given to man, allowing him to view his physical surroundings with the naked eye.

- **Our Spiritual Eyesight**: The word **typhlos** means seeing from a different perspective than from natural eyesight. This kind of vision provides a perspective unseen by the natural eye. It indicates a spiritual view beyond the physical and is a new perspective that was impossible to visualize before Christ made it available. This awareness of the unseen is necessary to allow us the ability to deal with the spiritual realm, be led by the Holy Spirit, equip ourselves with the armor of God, and identify the evil Satan throws our way.

In addition to seeing both physically and spiritually, we need to include a mental picture that broadens our minds and allows us to see beyond ourselves. The blindness from both the physical and spiritual requires the healing only the Lord can provide. Left to ourselves, we only see partially (natural eyesight), and all else remains unseen as we walk through life.

- **Our Mind (thinking)**: How we view and evaluate our surroundings and what we have available from the Lord to counteract the evil that wars against us. The evil that Satan is allowed to use against us is Satans attempt to keep us in the darkness and block the salvation God has intended for everyone (Remember 2 Corinthians 4:4 above).

Having physical blindness in this Scripture reveals that the Lord can open our physical eyes to see in the natural realm. But, this limits our ability to deal with our whole environment, and we are left blind to the spiritual realm. Partial vision leaves us unequipped to operate fully in the spiritual realm, and this is crippling as well as fatal to our future success.

What this means is that we need visibility for two different realms of operation. Again, our minds come into the picture because it only understands and is limited to the physical realm without a spiritual awakening. So, our thinking (Mind) is included in each process. The Lord must enact the spiritual aspect to receive the full awareness of our surroundings and the ability to visualize all that is present.

Scripture tells us that we need to renew our minds and incorporate the Word of God to obtain a better understanding (Romans 12:2). This spiritual vision occurs when we accept the Lord and receive the wisdom only He can provide to any given situation we encounter. Reading the Bible offers foundational truths with instructions that, along with the Holy Spirits' input, change our thinking.

Consider the following Scriptures to see further as the Lord increases your understanding and you contemplate and apply His principles to your everyday life:

2 Peter 1:9
*"But those who fail to develop in this way are shortsighted or blind (**typhlos**), forgetting that they have been cleansed from their old sins."*

2 Corinthians 4:4 (A repeat from earlier with more clarity)
*"Satan, who is the god of this world, has blinded (**typhlos**) the minds of those who don't believe. They are unable to see the glorious light of the Good News. They don't understand this message about the glories of Christ, who is the exact likeness of God."*

Remember Our Spiritual Foe

Ephesians 6:12
"For we are not fighting against flesh-and-blood enemies, but against evil rulers and authorities of the unseen (spiritual) world, against mighty powers in this dark world, and against evil spirits in the heavenly places."

Be Transformed in Your Thinking

Romans 12:2
"Don't copy the behavior and customs of this world, but <u>let God transform you into a new person by changing the way you think</u>. Then you will learn to know God's will for you, which is good and pleasing and perfect."

We must see beyond our natural eyesight because it limits our vision to only the physical realm. This one-sided visibility directly affects our thinking (limits). It sets the boundaries of our ability to best determine what is around us and how to deal with it successfully. Once we are given our spiritual eyes (accepting the Lord into our lives), we are given a vision into the spiritual realm. A spiritual awakening! Remember, our minds must be included to bring our thinking up to speed with what is happening around us.

Viewing life through both perspectives gives us the ability to encompass all involved in the world in which we live. Maintaining that there is only one perspective limits our ability to learn from God and does not renew our minds in the process. To incorporate God's wisdom and guidance into our lives, <u>we must see spiritually</u>. This spiritual vision is essential to grow and become more Christlike over time and receive the 'things' of God.

When we limit our possibilities, we remain in a diminished condition and unable to defend ourselves against the evil rulers and authorities that we encounter in the spiritual realm. We stay blind and cannot reason or see all that God has for us in the here and now.

Luke 4:16-21

"When he came to the village of Nazareth, his boyhood home, he went as usual to the synagogue on the Sabbath and stood up to read the Scriptures."

*'The scroll of Isaiah the prophet was handed to him. He unrolled the scroll and found the place where this was written: The Spirit of the Lord is upon me, for he has anointed me to bring Good News to the poor. He has sent me to proclaim that captives will be released, that the blind (**typhlos**) will see, that the oppressed will be set free, and that the time of the Lord's favor has come.'"*

"He rolled up the scroll, handed it back to the attendant, and sat down. All eyes in the synagogue looked at him intently. Then he began to speak to them. 'The Scripture you've just heard has been fulfilled this very day!'"

The response of the Pharisees was rejection, even to the point of trying to kill Jesus that very day. The Creator of the universe was physically standing in their presence where He told them they were witnessing a prophecy from Scripture in real-time in their very presence.

What was their reaction to this presentation the Lord was bringing to them? It was total rejection and denial of what they were witnessing (in the natural realm) because they were blind to the spiritual realm of reality that only God can bring into our existence.

The Pharisees had convinced themselves that their worldly knowledge and understanding were sufficient to comprehend what was happening around them. But, since what was happening had not been found in their accumulated knowledge of the Bible, they refused to believe. The direct result of their refusal to learn about God caused them to miss what the Lord had planned. Their salvation stood before them, but they would not receive the Truth.

Believing that salvation was provided through their knowledge of the Bible caused them to totally miss the coming of Christ. Rejection even when the Lord stood directly in front of them, reading Scripture aloud and relating that prophecy was being fulfilled at that very moment. What did the Pharisees do? Because they could not comprehend or see spiritually what was happening, they resisted the validity of the event. Their response revealed they were not open to anything other than what they thought (closed-minded) and believed.

The Pharisees chose to rely on their understanding and knowledge, limiting them from knowing the Truth of God and His Word. They just could not comprehend something more than they could physically see with the naked eye or reason (understand) in their unspiritual minds.

This mindset caused them to completely miss the Lord as He stood in their midst and fulfilled the very prophecy He was reading in their presence. Without the Lord removing the scale from our eyes, it shows that our ability leaves us in darkness. The darkness is where Satan operates, and that is where the devil wants us to stay.

Scripture Gives Warning about Spiritual Blindness

Luke 11:35
"Make sure that the light you think you have is not actually darkness."

Ephesians 4:18
"Their minds are full of darkness; they wander far from the life God gives because they have closed their minds and hardened their hearts against him."

1 John 1:6
"So we are lying if we say we have fellowship with God but go on living in spiritual darkness; we are not practicing the truth."

God Wants Us to Spiritually Connect with Him and Grow in Faith

2 Peter 1:3-11

"By his divine power, God has given us everything we need for living a godly life. We have received all of this by coming to know him, the one who called us to himself by means of his marvelous glory and excellence."

"And because of his glory and excellence, he has given us great and precious promises. These are the promises that enable you to share his divine nature and escape the world's corruption caused by human desires."

"In view of all this, make every effort to respond to God's promises. Supplement your faith with a generous provision of moral excellence, and moral excellence with knowledge, and knowledge with self-control, and self-control with patient endurance, and patient endurance with godliness, and godliness with brotherly affection, and brotherly affection with love for everyone."

"The more you grow like this, the more productive and useful you will be in your knowledge of our Lord Jesus Christ. But those who fail to develop in this way are shortsighted or blind (spiritually blind), forgetting that they have been cleansed from their old sins."

"So, dear brothers and sisters, work hard to prove that you really are among those God has called and chosen. Do these things, and you will never fall away. Then God will give you a grand entrance into the eternal Kingdom of our Lord and Savior Jesus Christ."

Without the Lord in our lives, we are powerless to proceed toward Him and see all that He has made available. The visibility of humankind without the Lord is minimal. We will discover our mind is void of the true wisdom of God, and our way of thinking WILL NOT provide us with access to the Lord no matter how hard we try. A total effort in futility is our inevitable outcome, including all the rotten fruit that accompanies such a decision.

It could be summed up in very few words, and no one would like to be at your side or reap all the difficulties that will be the direct results. Now, if your future is dependent on your doings, I would highly suggest that you make a change (choose) and trust in the Lord and better your current situation for a much more favorable and enjoyable life. Remember, spiritual blindness leaves you in spiritual darkness and without the Lord's guidance.

When you read about healings in Scripture, you will soon find that Jesus healed many that were physically blind and could not see. You will also see in several applications that He healed those who were spiritually blind as well. They could see very well in the physical sense, but they were blind to spiritual things.

Scripture tells us that we must accept the Lord to become saved to have our spiritual eyes opened. And that we are spiritually dead until we do so. That action of faith on our part equates to complete visibility once we choose to accept the Lord's salvation package (Romans 3:25).

There is no other way to see spiritually until we make a choice to accept Him as our Lord and Savior. The Pharisees refused to receive anything Jesus offered because they had made their minds up that what was taking place in front of them did not logically make sense. How could the coming of Christ, the Messiah, take place like this? It wasn't unfolding the way they thought it should take place, so they rejected it.

Do you have your mindset on how 'things' are supposed to happen and are blinded to what is really going on? A mistake of this nature is not unusual and happens all the time. Our reluctance to accept Christ is widespread, but if left unchecked, it could keep you in the dark and cause you to remain there your entire life.

Mark 16:16
"Anyone who believes and is baptized will be saved. But anyone who refuses to believe will be condemned."

John 1:12-13
"But to all who believed him and accepted him, he gave the right to become children of God. And anyone who believes in God's Son has eternal life. Anyone who doesn't obey the Son will never experience eternal life but remains under God's angry judgment."

How is your vision in the realm of reality — the real world? Are you 'seeing' with the natural eye only, or have you been healed by the Lord to experience and protect yourself from the spiritual forces that are all around you? The position of where you are in life, a believer or a nonbeliever, and how you receive or reject this reality will determine your present condition and future. Please check yourself and realistically approach this question with persistent prayer and find out for yourself and be sure.

Many people have instantly rejected what is in front of them only to find out their understanding was incorrect later. God has provided each believer with spiritual vision and the ability to 'see' with new eyes, reason with a whole new knowledge, and provide wisdom never before understood.

Don't restrict your visibility by allowing your limited understanding to block the possibilities provided in Scripture. Be available to see what is possible with the anointing of the Holy Spirit active in your life. Putting aside something you don't first understand may be blocking your future from receiving all that God has planned for your life.

Once we turn toward the Lord, we find He understands our human condition. He has made provisions to move us out of darkness (spiritual blindness) and into His glorious light. His light reveals the sin in our lives, and some do not want to risk the revealing of their sins — so they refuse His offer.

This, too, is normal, but we must choose and push on if we are serious about becoming a believer. We must accept Christ to benefit from all He offers. He has granted our independence as part of our free will. We are given the right by God to make our own choices and choose for ourselves. God does warn us what we will reap should we choose to remain alone and not follow after Him.

In putting God to the side, we have made our choice to go through life alone. Remember that the consequences that follow are certain to bring failure and an eternity doomed by its location and the punishment that will undoubtedly follow.

God did not create humankind to send them to eternal damnation. He created humanity and gave us the free will to choose in life as we desire. This free will was also provided so we could choose Him and receive the salvation He made available through His Son.

The redemption Christ provided was made very simple and accessible to all that would accept it. As you read Scripture, you will soon discover that humankind without the Lord yields no godly fruit. Because this was well known, God provided a way to freely choose Him and escape the punishment of sin in the world we were born into.

Pray with Me: Lord, show me personally the reality of my decisions and the results. Please save me from an end full of regret and sorrow. Open my eyes to your fullness and cause me to desire and follow after You. I realize I need your help in doing what's right. I know I'm weak without you, and I choose to follow You so I can become the person you created me to be. Thank you, Lord. Amen

Chapter 2

Can I Determine How I'm Doing So Far?

I like it when the Lord drops a new idea into my mind. Today I was sitting on the couch thinking about the possibility of projecting our personal life into a scale that would evaluate and help us visualize our cooperation with the Lord. Almost immediately, He gave me an idea that satisfied my question. It was much different from what I would typically imagine and brought excitement to my spirit.

He showed me a bar scale and how to do a self-evaluation regarding our obedience to Scripture. It will provide a picture of where we function in God's sight based on our living life on the earth. Are you ready? Well, here it is anyway.

If you want to explain something, it is good to measure it visually. Maybe you need to cut a piece of wood to length to accomplish building a piece of furniture. Or, perhaps you want to sew together a blouse with the many different components. To achieve making the blouse would require each piece to be made to a specific dimension to have an item be a specified size upon completion.

There is nothing unusual about that logical way of thinking. But, if you were to measure something not tangible, how would you determine a way to visualize a nonphysical object that you could not see, touch or feel? That is where the scale I'm going to present comes into play. So, here goes.

Let's use a bar chart and focus on a scale to try and visualize our percent of obedience to the Lord. Take a look at the following chart. It determines you are being obedient to the Lord 80 percent of the time. Another believer's obedience is set at 50 percent. The following chart would look something like this:

This bar chart will reveal the percentage of your actions in obedience based on the choices you make in compliance to Scripture. We will use 5 of the Ten Commandments from the bible to accumulate this

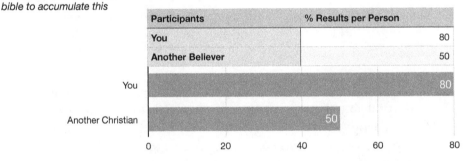

The above bar chart will give you a visual that reflects your performance compared to another believer based on your percentage of obedience to each Scripture that follows. Making this comparison will reflect a percentage of obedience — for each individual. This percentage would involve each person viewing their daily routine and then evaluating their actions compared to the five scriptural verses noted.

- First, let's look at **the 3rd Commandment** and determine how you line up with its instructions. The third commandment reads: *"Thou shall not take the name of the Lord thy God in vain."*

I heard my grandma say a bad word once. She told me it was a bad word and that she should not have said it. I didn't know until then it was a bad word because I had to clean out the milk stall one time and the product being removed was common throughout the whole coral where the livestock was fed, watered, and the cattle came in from the pasture to eat and drink.

Now, if my grandma only said this word once, I would say she had a pretty good handle on her tongue. Especially since I'm currently in my seventies, about her age when she slipped, and could not claim I was even close to her one-time slip up. I was in the Marine Corps, and many more words were used — even some I'd never heard before, and I was 20-years old at the time.

Anyway, if I were to compare myself to my grandma, I would fail miserably, and it probably would prove that I needed to be taken back out behind the woodshed an extra time or two. There are other things a lot worse I did where the woodshed would apply that didn't even come to anyone's attention.

So, how's your vocabulary compared to the third commandment? You're probably closer to me than my grandma, so we'll move on to the next Scripture. Have you improved over the years and grown more able to guard your mouth? Hopefully, you are growing in the Lord and exercising self-control with His help. Keep in mind Scripture regarding this area — like:

Psalm 34:13
"Then keep your tongue from speaking evil and your lips from telling lies!"

So, on a scale from 1 to 100, evaluate yourself and mark where you're at on the bar chart. If you are improving with age, this is a good thing. If you're not, it's time to visit with the Lord and get His help.

- A second reference is **the 4th Commandment:** *"Remember to observe the Sabbath day by keeping it holy."* See how you line up with this commandment that God has given.

Hebrews 10:25
"And let us not neglect our meeting together, as some people do, but encourage one another, especially now that the day of his return is drawing near."

How do you evaluate your life when reading this verse? Do you attend church, or do you find other activities to fill this time frame? I do not intend a rigid religious can't miss a Sunday guideline here. I'm asking if you purposely do not attend any activity with other Christians, avoid meeting on purpose, shy away from fellowship to refresh your biblical beliefs, and find activities you would rather do? Any reactions to your obedience as you determine your personal actions? How'd you do?

What do you see yourself scoring on this command? If you attend only on holidays, then you are a CEO. That means that you participate at Christmas, Easter, and Other special events only. So that you know, that's not very high when it comes to the percentage of obedience— just say'n. Don't keep a score of how many times you attend church each year, but do determine if you regularly attend as a general rule.

God desires that we fellowship with other believers and are involved in supporting our church financially and regularly (Hebrews 10:25). That congregation will most likely need your function in the church you attend to complete their ministry in serving the Lord. Maybe you are supportive on the prayer team and pray for people at the altar. Praying for others is a tremendous blessing, and it provides you the opportunity to lift and agree in prayer with other believers in their time of need and thankfulness.

Whatever your participation maybe will be an intricate part of the whole church and benefit others greatly. Our commitment to serving the Lord causes us to grow and flourish in our walk with Him. Our involvement added to the fullness necessary to reach an unsaved world will build our understanding and increase our faith in the Lord.

Speaking of God's Word is critical as the Lord strengthens our progress in becoming more familiar with Him and learning to function outside the fellowship that is needed to help us in our walk with Him.

If you're going regularly and learning and growing in the Lord, you are following God's desire for you. Evaluate yourself from all you see taking place in your life. Don't base your score on numbers — base your percentage on how you are doing overall. Are you just hanging in there, or are you growing closer to the Lord over time?

- Let's look at a third reference — **the 5th Commandment**, and see how you measure up: *"Honor thy father and thy mother."* Please don't confuse the fifth as a means to plead 'no comment' or anything that would indicate you are innocent. Let's get honest and review how you really did in your lifetime — especially up to right now!

Do you honor your parents? It does not matter how you were treated by them growing up. What matters is, do you honor them according to Scripture or not? Do you have a checklist with all their failures and how they should have treated you at home? Even if they were a negative force in your life, they are still YOUR parents.

I was not fond of my father early on because he was angry most of the time. He was angry toward us all, and it was not a secret. He could have done much better as a father, but he also had many great qualities he passed on to us all, which I benefit from even today. It does not matter that he was angry because that's not an excuse for me to have been dishonoring.

I took to heart from the Bible as a child that we are to honor our father and mother. Of course, I did not like or agree all the time and had issues later in life that stemmed from his expression of anger in how

I conducted my own life. That experience was not an excuse the Bible allowed because I thought I had just cause. Certainly not!

Scripture provides several nuggets of wisdom that require our obedience, and they tell us why. The Bible isn't just a book of suggestions for us to reflect on and then do whatever feels good. It is a book of instructions to follow so we maximize our efforts in the right direction and benefit from them. Just look at the following several verses:

Deuteronomy 5:16
"Honor your father and mother, as the Lord your God commanded you. Then you will live a long, full life in the land the Lord your God is giving you."

Luke 18:20
"But to answer your question, you know the commandments: 'You must not commit adultery. You must not murder. You must not steal. You must not testify falsely. Honor your father and mother.'"

Ephesians 6:1
"Children, obey your parents because you belong to the Lord, for this is the right thing to do."

So what if you don't honor your father and mother — no matter what the reason? God knows this is an area in life that requires our attention. This command requires us to purpose and choose to follow God's Word rather than emotions. Some have good reasons for feeling contrary to this command. Feelings are not an excuse to be disobedient. To honor others when we believe we have good reason to dishonor them is not acceptable with God.

Remaining disobedient to this command opens the door to very harmful activities to enter into our lives and paves a future path that misses out on God's best for us. There is good reason to honor our parents and learn that discipline is necessary to receive all God intends to bless you in life.

Maybe you have children who disrespect you because they feel a certain way about your carrying out your role as a parent. It might be you did the best you knew how at the time, but room for improvement opened a gap for evil to enter from your child's point of view. Their perspective may need your careful attention!

I remember when visiting with my wife and two children about an incident in our family where we were all directly involved. As we each discussed our viewpoints of the situation, my son relayed how differently the incident had appeared to him. It was precisely the opposite of how the other three saw this same event. It caused me to be more open to the feelings of others because I could easily see how he evaluated the circumstances and came to his conclusion after hearing his reasoning.

It was something I'd never thought about before. This discussion caused me to be more prayerful and open to the feelings of others and not assume everyone else arrived at the same conclusion as me because I thought a certain way. I learned that the same circumstances could yield very different conclusions. That individual's evaluation was based on their viewpoint — not mine. And, usually, how we feel about a situation dominates that individual's interpretation of the entire matter and how they respond.

I learned from that experience and have reflected on it several times during my life. I always want others to be uplifted and encouraged by what I discuss, but there may be times I don't come across that way. Looking back, I can see where I could have done much better. It is now my responsibility to improve over time as I allow the Lord to change me. That simple choice can make all the difference to each new situation.

Honoring your parents is an excellent start to respecting others even when you don't feel like it. This choice doesn't mean you ignore the negative, but it does mean you need to honor God and His Word and capitalize on the positive during this time. There will always be something positive about a person, and we each need to focus on what's good — and not focus only on the negative.

Ephesians 6:2-3

"Honor your father and mother. This is the first commandment with a promise. If you honor your father and mother, 'things will go well for you, and you will have a long life on the earth.'"

Philippians 4:8

"Fix your thoughts on what is true, and honorable, and right, and pure, and lovely, and admirable. Think about things that are excellent and worthy of praise."

Praying for Others is a Form of Worship

1 Timothy 2:1

"I urge you, first of all, to pray for all people. Ask God to help them; intercede on their behalf, and give thanks for them."

Remain in prayer for those around you and lift them up to the Lord. They, too, have areas, just like we do, and they need our mercy and prayers to reach a closer relationship with the Lord. Humankind is not perfect, nor will it ever be. That includes all of us, and I appreciate those praying for me because it presses me forward and closer to the Lord.

God's extension of grace and mercy to all humankind is a beautiful opportunity to allow Him to work in and through us (Philippians 4:8). Since I am aware that I need His help, I want to receive all I can while I'm still here among the living. The end isn't in sight quite yet, but I am aware it will be in my future. Death is a 100% guarantee that is certain to everyone living. Its arrival, the end, can be exciting because it opens up our portal to enter Eternity with the Lord for each believer!

I've believed these Scriptures to honor my parents my whole life, and I was determined to follow them no matter what. Why? Because I did not want the consequences that come from being disobedient. I did fear what God might do if I didn't obey. I can remember as a child having my feelings repeatedly hurt because of my dad's anger. I also remember praying for my father's salvation, and God would save him even though he acted this way. I seemed to always see a good result for him, and it came — but many years later in life.

Guess what? My father sold out to the Lord towards the end of his life, and I believe the Lord allowed me to be a part of his acceptance of salvation. I was going to visit him when I was an adult, and I slowed down to turn into the driveway. I looked up, and he was fixing a small boy's bicycle in the garage. I chose to drive on and watch from a distance. The Lord gave me a soothing ointment for my boyhood wounds that day as I watched my father do a good deed for a young boy from next door. Something that he would never have taken the time for when I was young.

That picture is still in my mind today, and I got to see a changed man that happened to be my father. It brought joy to my heart and healing to my soul that I didn't completely understand at the time. It did, however, cause me to open up my heart and receive his kindness into my being like he was doing it for me. The Lord was working on me, too, and I was enjoying the healing results.

The Lord revealed to me the root of the problem with my father. It was a wound from his past that needed healing. I'm sure the Lord had been working on him for some time, but I had hoped to be the one that would pray with him in this area. Life doesn't usually work out exactly the way we want, but God still completes His work in that person in His timing.

He went home to be with the Lord before I was able to pray with him, but his manner of actions and attention toward me had changed so much over our final years together. I cherished our friendship together for his last ten years. Every ill-feeling between us had evaporated during that time, and we became good friends before he passed.

After my dad was put to rest, we gathered at our farmhouse in Oklahoma. My dad's sister came to me and asked if I knew why my dad became interested in the Lord. I told her I did not know. She proceeded to tell me that my example of following after the Lord caused him to seek the Lord for himself. He had always thought this God thing was not for real, but watching me change over the years made him realize it was a relationship and not a religion.

I was overwhelmed with delight as I listened to her tell me this story. I had not realized until she relayed what he had told her that I made a difference in my dad's life that caused him to seek the Lord. What a wonderful gift to give me when I needed it the most.

I think my reward for choosing to honor him opened the way for our friendship to blossom because I got out of the way of the Lord working in his life. Had I remained bitter and unforgiving and not honored him, I believe the end of his life might have remained harsh and full of rejection, and my ill feelings would have remained an opposing force in both our lives!

You can look back at your life, determine how well you did in this area, and give yourself a percentage for obedience. Just remember, we all start at 0% and hopefully improve over the years and learn why Scripture in action brings God's wisdom into practical applications in our lives. He will bring it as we dive into His Word and pray for wisdom to head in the direction He designates for each individual (Proverbs 2:1-21; Proverbs 3:18; Proverbs 4:7 & 8; Proverbs 8:12).

- Consider a fourth reference — **the 8th Commandment**: *"Thou shall not steal."*

Does looking back during your life cause any memories to surface? It certainly did for me. Just this past week, I was reminded of a stolen combination lock. I stole this combination lock when I was in junior high from a drug store not far away. I found the combination written on a piece of cardboard located in my nightstand.

It was a Master Lock I needed for my school hall locker. I wanted it but didn't want to spend my money to purchase it. I thought it was a little too expensive, so I stole it and used it throughout high school until I graduated. Today I use it on a chain that locks my motorcycle trailer to a fixed object when I travel and stay in a motel overnight on the way to and from when traveling on the road. It's my security lock against someone stealing my Harley and trailer while spending the night in a motel. Isn't that an interesting use for a stolen lock? The stolen lock is being used to secure something of value to me from being stolen. What a thought!

Now that's fantastic usage for a stolen lock and certainly has served me well all these many years. The only problem is that I stole it, and when I finally felt guilty, which was many years later, I could not take it back because the store was long gone, and I was left holding the stolen merchandise. I asked the Lord to forgive me, and He did. I've stopped stealing since then, so the problem has not reoccurred in my life.

So, I started with a negative percentage of obedience many years ago. But, I have raised my percentage since then. So now, I should average it out over the 61 years since this occurred? Well, I should be at a much higher bar chart percentage now than when I was young. And, if I factor in that God remembers our sins no more after we ask for forgiveness — then, I can now put myself at 81% on my bar chart without any problem or possible repercussions.

Technically, I could move my percentage to 100% if I followed the Lord's example and forgot it altogether and remembered it no more. More learning on my part is necessary to forget all of my past wrong-doings and fully follow His example.

This 'forgetting' is Spiritual Folks — Take a Look at two Bible verses that State this very Thing

1 John 1:9
"But if we confess our sins to him, he is faithful and just to forgive us our sins and to cleanse us from all wickedness (unrighteousness)."

Hebrews 8:12
"And I will forgive their wickedness, and I will never again remember their sins."

Forgiveness from the Lord is final and forgotten. God chooses to forget our forgiven sins and places them on a horizontal plane that projects them into infinity. God says He takes our sins as far away from us as the East is from the West (Psalm 103:12). Then, He remembers them no more. This means our sins totally disappear and are removed forever — never to be remembered by Him again.

Sometimes we keep bringing them up and realize we have not released our sin completely. As we grow in wisdom and knowledge of the Lord, we'll find our memory also needs the cleansing forgiveness provides. Shouldn't we also forget our past sins, rejoice in the Lord for His forgiveness, and enjoy the peace that forgiveness brings?

I believe the forgiveness of God is final and that we should follow His example and not feel guilty for past forgiven sins. Remembering a past forgiven wrong is a lesson learned and is good for our gratefulness, but don't let it continue to plague you with sorrow. God didn't condition us to carry our wrongdoings (baggage) the rest of our lives. That's why forgiveness is critical for our advancement in the Lord!

I believe when I read that His burden is light in Scripture, He is referring to the forgiveness of sin and that our journey in life can be much easier with Him rather than dealing with all life brings on our own. Carrying guilt throughout life is not what God wants for us. We are not designed to pack around this extra burden.

Guilt does have a purpose, and that is to bring us into the right relationship with the Lord and cause us to turn to Him and receive the gift of forgiveness He offers. A life that is burdened with sin and unforgiveness becomes increasingly burdensome and more challenging to manage the longer we wait to call upon Him (1 John 1:9).

Look at Additional Scripture Regarding Sin

1 John 1:5-10
"This is the message we heard from Jesus and now declare to you: God is light, and there is no darkness in him at all."

"So we are lying if we say we have fellowship with God but go on living in spiritual darkness; we are not practicing the truth."

"But if we are living in the light, as God is in the light, then we have fellowship with each other, and the blood of Jesus, his Son, cleanses us from all sin."

"If we claim we have no sin, we are only fooling ourselves and not living in the truth."

"<u>But if we confess our sins to him, he is faithful and just to forgive us our sins and to cleanse us from all wickedness</u>."

"If we claim we have not sinned, we are calling God a liar and showing that his word has no place in our hearts."

God is a <u>Way Maker</u>, and the forces working against us and what we are up against He is well aware. Because of that knowledge, He has provided a way to unload our many sorrows and sins. Sins that clutter our lives as we journey through our time on earth. His care and love for us exceed our natural thinking because He does not want us to trudge through life on our own.

It is difficult to understand the love (agape) of God because it is so different from what we can experience on our own (physical love). Unconditional love (agape) does not hold back when we do something wrong. It doesn't judge us because we aren't perfect. It is always available and always welcoming, even when we aren't so lovable. Even when we have sinned against Him — His forgiveness is always available. His love never changes! That is the beauty of Agape love. It is the nature of God, and it never changes or is conditional.

As you look at your own life regarding sin, how are you doing? Are you ignoring sin in your own life and carrying around the guilt (heavy baggage)? If you are operating in this mode, you are stealing from yourself the peace that God provides that comes with forgiveness. Do yourself a favor and reach out and grasp the forgiveness the Lord offers and give yourself relief from this burden of guilt. God's way has tremendous benefits that you can experience and lighten your load on your way to eternity.

Take another reference from Scripture and determine your activities based on its message. Look at **the 9th Commandant**: *"Thou shall not bear false witness against thy neighbor."*

This Commandment seems to be regularly neglected by humankind on a large scale. Remembering back in your life, did you ever hear a story about someone that not only seemed logical, based on what you had witnessed personally but seemed logical without further discussion? You had imagined this story yourself in your mind, and hearing it from someone else just confirmed your feelings.

This thinking and conversation quickly becomes gossip and should be avoided. Maybe you've had someone tell a story about you, but it did not line up with the truth of the situation. Had they been present, they would have known better, but because it seemed logical to you, no verification was sought or seemed necessary?

Then, when you shared the 'story' with others, the rumor spread and caught fire. The fire burned in the minds of many, and you believed it because a reliable person had given you the details with color images that you accepted completely — without question. After all, it seemed plausible.

Now, what if the story you heard was not true? What if it had been fabricated and embellished with details that intrigued your imagination. Once your desire to tell someone else took place, it ignited a fire that spread quickly, with almost everyone believing the false implication of details. Now, what do you think about this now vicious rumor that has been told as if it were true? Can you understand the damage a story like this would do to an individual's reputation?

And, how would you defend yourself if you were the victim? Your defense would be impossible because the lies were passed on to who knows who, and you couldn't retrieve the untrue statements even if you wanted to. The fire has been started, and the flames are blazing and burning like a forest fire. Your neglect to confirm the truth while telling others makes you a part of the lie. You may have even chosen to believe the spreading gossip because your motive was to hurt the other person.

A match or spark can start a fire in the forest and burn many acres of trees, and it may take a thousand firefighters to finally get it put out. But that's a forest fire, and we're talking about rumors. The wind of gossip can become very forceful, and it only fans the spread of the fire way beyond the flame that started the whole blaze. And the final results bring great destruction to all in its path. The damage is not only to the person, but it causes widespread damage to anything in its path with no way to put out the raging, out of control burning fire.

The 9th Commandment is quite sobering when you project what damage a false witness can cause by contributing to something not checked out for validity. A person's moral character will suffer greatly, and when the truth becomes knowledgable, it will reveal that each participant will undoubtedly have a part in the destruction that has resulted.

In this day and age, we must be cautious about what we post on the internet regarding another person. Our feelings should be filtered, so we are not participating in becoming a false witness or to a lie of untruth. We have a responsibility for our actions, and we should be careful how we transfer a thought and present it as a truth. Be very careful! There are sobering consequences that follow after spreading a false rumor about another person.

Gossip is a tool used by our advisory, the devil, to destroy others and reap destruction to all humanity as possible. Our responsibility is to be certain what we say is truth, or we should remain quiet rather than join with Satan's team to cause the vicious rumor that assists him as he lashes out to steal, kill, and destroy!

As we view our actions in life and compare them with the Word of God, we can get a good picture of ourselves. This self-portrait of who we are provides us with a snapshot of our overall percentage of obedience. It also provides a picture of how easily our natural thinking can become a destroyer serving the ruler of this world — Satan, rather than God! Obedience is what the Lord prefers from each of us.

Proverbs 16:28
"A perverse man sows strife, And a whisperer separates the best of friends."

Proverbs 19:9
"A false witness will not go unpunished, And he who speaks lies shall perish."

1 Timothy 5:13
"And besides they learn to be idle, wandering about from house to house, and not only idle but also gossips and busybodies, saying things which they ought not."

Our words project what we believe in our hearts and overflow to those around us. God does not approve of gossip or being a false witness that spreads rumors. Trouble for all involved comes as a result and places a temptation for others to falter. Don't fall prey to the temptation to speak about another without first consulting Scripture. Your answer and suggested response are woven throughout the Bible.

Knowing that we cannot be all that God wants us to be alone is the beginning of wisdom and will enhance our thinking on our journey through life. Our realization of ourselves and how we are is essential to identify ourselves and our character in the world. God has made Himself available, through Jesus Christ, to provide a means to travel life by utilizing God's wisdom and Helper (the Holy Spirit) to get us through in the best possible condition with all the help we need to become more Christlike.

Becoming more Christlike can be achieved as a believer in Jesus by continuing to learn and grow in God's Truth as His principles are practiced all along the way. It's a lifetime adventure with perks and benefits during the entire journey with an eternal destination of Heaven when all our time is exhausted here.

How do I become a believer? Becoming a believer is the means to grasp this possibility. All you need is to accept the Lord into your life. The following prayer will bring you into this way of life and give you the help you need to start your journey with Him and partake of all He has to offer.

———————+———————

Pray out Loud to the Lord:

Jesus, I am a sinner. I am sorry for all that I have done wrong. I repent of the sins in my life (lying, stealing, cursing, lusting, coveting, jealousy, hatefulness, what I was born into, etc.), and I accept what you (Jesus) did by dying on the cross in my place. I ask you to come into my heart and 'change me' into a new creation.' Give me the spiritual eyes to see and the ability to hear your voice as you take me on the path that you have planned for me even before the beginning of time. Cleanse me by your shed blood and fill me with your Holy Spirit. I want to serve you and grow into the person you created me to be. Help me be all that I was created for and to fulfill my destiny in you. I ask this in Jesus' name, Amen.

———————+———————

Think about this Verse —

Isaiah 30:18

"So the Lord must wait for you to come to him so he can show you his love and compassion. For the Lord is a faithful God. Blessed are those who wait for his help."

Chapter 3

Are You a Partial Believer?

Choosing to accept Christ as your Savior and Lord make you a believer. You are now a child of the living God. You are now a recipient of all the benefits Christ obtained when He died in our place on the cross. This prayer of acceptance is extended to all humanity. It gives each of us accessibility to God and receives His help during our journey on earth.

So now we're going to address your level of commitment to the Lord. And how well you follow after His leading. How is this done? Well, we first need to get into reading His Word — the Bible. The Bible is His written information containing godly wisdom and divine instruction. The Word provides many stories of past believers as they went through their struggles, failures, and victories. We can obtain a great deal of wisdom from their experiences that still speak to us today.

They were human just like we are and had many similar problems that still exist in our culture. Their actions are recorded for our instruction from which to learn. If we can apply His Word and see how to act and how not to react, it will provide many opportunities for us to succeed and avoid many pitfalls.

Some folks look at the Bible as a list of do's and don't. It is actually a storybook written by man through the empowerment of the Holy Spirit, giving humankind a better way to approach living and have the best opportunity to be successful (Joshua 1:8). God wants us to prosper and to enjoy our time on earth. We aren't placed here to struggle independently and only exist the best we can until death.

The Bible provides principles that work in every generation with instruction that applies to any culture or situation. The wisdom is timeless and never loses its effectiveness when used. God promises us that when we apply His Word and complete our part of the instructions, we will prosper and have good success (Psalm 1:1-3). The Bible is quite an instruction book we have available, and applying its principles will benefit us greatly as we experience life first-hand.

To define a partial believer is to view a person that only applies Scripture to their lives when they feel pressure from life's burdens; or, maybe react to God's instruction once in a while but not in each opportunity. It could be a situation not deemed important enough, so they don't apply the principle given in His Word and avoid confrontation altogether. This kind of wisdom is made available by God and our participation reveals our free will to exercise this freedom by choosing for ourselves.

Let's take, for example, tithing. This area has much resistance from most people. I didn't want to tithe in the beginning because I felt I could not afford to. I had been unemployed for 11 months and could not return to my former occupation because of a medical condition. Because logically, based on my reasoning at that time, I was in great need of employment and a steady income — not more expenses.

Once I became employed, I had to start with a lower hourly wage because I could not return to my former profession that yielded a much better income. This new beginning limited my earnings and caused me to work for less if I wanted a job at all. Construction was what I was good at, but now I had to eliminate all physical work.

I had all these bills due, like everyone else, and needed every dime I could make to not only pay the current ones but to catch up on past debts incurred during the 11 months of sickness. Changing professions caused me to start over in a new field, and I had no experience to help me. When it came to my new income, there was much less available, and tithing was not logical from my perspective at all.

That was my excuse anyway. It didn't make sense to give money away when it was already in short supply. Tithing was not a consideration I was open to or willing to apply. Why in the world would you give money away when you didn't have enough, to begin with? I thought that was a stupid idea even though it was discussed in detail in the Bible (Malachi 3:8-10). This principle was not logical at all!

Well, the Lord got a hold of me, and I started reading about tithing, but I remained resistant to what Scripture had to say. The more I read, the more I began to understand some of the ideas behind it better, but it still didn't set with my logical thinking anymore now than before. Because God's way was not reasonable, I continued to live my way and not apply this biblical principle.

As time went on, I finally gave in to a partial tithe but still not all the way. You might say I had withdrawal systems. That is, I was feeling the pain in my billfold each time I contributed money to the offering plate. I even considered making change out of the offering plate if I had a larger bill than the amount I wanted to give. That was an obvious sign of withdrawal that I struggled with for some time in the future. God's system of tithing and the reason for it seemed utterly unrealistic.

Anyway, as I grew in the Lord, the better I got until I reached ten percent. Ten percent after bills were paid, that is — still partial. I heard a person ask our pastor once to give ten percent of our gross or net income. I was sure I was doing the right thing by paying tithing from the net amount. Then the pastor's answer came, and I heard him say: "It depends on whether you want a net blessing or a gross blessing. It's your choice."

That got to me because I thought I had come so far in getting where I could tithe off the net income. As you might guess, I discovered I wanted the gross blessing on a net tithe. So, I prayed and asked for forgiveness for my little faith and upped the tithe to ten percent of my gross.

As I learned more about tithing and heard others give testimony of their finances, I marveled at the changes they told. I saw in Malachi how the Lord wanted us to test Him, and that intrigued me to give Him a chance. As I followed His Word wholly, I soon learned the significant changes that followed in resolving my financial difficulties. From that point on, I learned that testing the Lord in this area was something I did not fully understand but realized it worked. Finally, I found peace regarding my tithing issues, and now maybe the Lord and I could work on something else. And we did!

I also learned that I was a partial believer because if I disagreed with what Scripture was showing me in other areas — I would do it my way instead. My little faith needed a great deal of overhauling and a great deal of growth. It just so happened the Lord was very willing to reveal to me my wrong thinking. Life is much more difficult if you even occasionally insist on your way. And besides, inserting your free will allows us to avoid issues in our reluctance to respond to the Lord. And, our avoidance will always let you learn the hard way — if you insist.

Maybe free will has a downside? Yes, it does, and I had to discover that reality on my own. Resistant believers are a hard bunch to indoctrinate with the wisdom of God. Why? Because our natural thinking can provide options that seem best and easier. I'm slow at learning, but I am doing much better now that I'm more mature. I'm now older and finally available to the Lord — full-time. It didn't take me a whole lifetime to learn this — just most of it!

How do you see yourself? It may take a close friend or spouse to clear your vision. We are so prone to be more critical of others than we are of ourselves. And, many times, we don't see ourselves the same as we look at others. Our self-protective mechanism is a natural guard

43

(pride) that we build around ourselves to ward off those who differ in our thinking and lifestyle.

That protective covering (pride) deflects the outside world and provides us with enough protection to get comfortable with the way things are. Besides, most of us don't like change because we get comfortable where we are and don't relish adjusting our behavior or attitude. The problem then is deciding to remain comfortable, but that does not provide any opportunity to grow or expand our current condition and grow in the wisdom of God.

The free will the Lord gives us always provides an option. We can choose what the Bible recommends or not. The difficulty could be because the solution may seem logically ridiculous and also uncomfortable. The good thing is realizing our natural human condition (pride) but choosing to step out in faith anyway.

We will only be uncomfortable for a while and find a solution that releases us from our current condition. Then, when we come into the light of Scripture and discover the rewards of our actions produces excellent benefits. The short-lived discomfort is soon forgotten when weighted against the godly results. It is a welcomed relief that resolves our initial problem and brings a solution that eliminates the root cause.

The light of truth found in the Bible is a wonderful way to develop a realistic view of ourselves. Having others around you that are caring but honest in helping you evaluate your spiritual walk is very comforting and provides excellent support during your lifetime. The moments of discomfort are then shared and allow us to realize we are all very much alike. Battling life with help is a great place to grow and flourish.

When I was in Vietnam, the Marine Corps told us that it took ten personnel behind the front line to support every person in combat. I don't know how this ratio works today, but it encouraged me to find myself in a group that others were helping support even though I did not encounter them personally.

Just after I arrived in Vietnam, I learned the Navy had recently provided warm water so we could shower in comfort. Milk and meat were served every Sunday in the mess hall, and we had a tin-roofed hootch to sleep in to protect us from the elements. The hootch also had screens wrapped all-around to ward off insects. These were luxuries given our situation, and I very much appreciated each one of them.

Looking at your present situation and condition, can you determine your position from a realistic viewpoint? How do you measure your growth in the Lord? Are you more obedient today than you were a year ago? Are you satisfied with your selections in life when you view the results? What is your standing regarding eternity? What if tomorrow all changed? How would you fare with all that directly affects you currently?

Life is jam-packed with elements that require a choice, and the collective decisions you've made place you where you are today. Your selections also help determine the quality of your lifestyle and certainly where you will spend eternity. Your current circumstances represent all your collective choices, and you will need to respond to each of them from God's perspective if you want your outcome to be the very best.

I'm not talking about your social level, country of origin, the color of your skin, but I am talking about how you have responded to life's difficulties and how you have selected the next step to take in moving forward with your time spent here. Each challenge is an opportunity to incorporate God's principles in your actions and apply them to your circumstances. Each obstacle is another opportunity to select God's way and see for yourself just how valuable His wisdom turns out (Matthew 11:19).

He clearly tells us in Scripture that certain choices will end in failure, and He also explains that certain other choices will end in victory. Hence, His guidelines have a purpose and provide His help in resolving any issues when applied. Choosing requires our attention to either move forward based on our knowledge or choose to trust by faith His principles to resolve the current situation.

Check This Scripture from the Old Testament Because it Still Applies Today

Deuteronomy 30:19

"Today I have given you the choice between life and death, between blessings and curses. Now I call on heaven and earth to witness the choice you make. Oh, that you would choose life, so that you and your descendants might live!"

It is man's tendency to venture out on his own and give it a try to see if his knowledge will work. I believe our inquiring minds need to experience our thinking and see if it will work without God's intervention. This idea seemed logical to me because I'm inquisitive and would like to find out for myself. I never figured I needed anybody to help me move forward, so trying it on my own, at first, seemed best.

Little did I know the Lord had been through this selfish endeavor many times with other individuals. I wasn't His first, nor would I be His last independent traveler. He just wanted me to trust Him, apply His principles, and see for myself there was help available and a real need for Him. Trusting Scripture takes time, and growing in faith takes longer than I had hoped. Depending on Him can be a challenge your whole life. I'm learning to grow in trust in Him almost every day because when a new opportunity arises, I have to pause and remember who's the Creator and who is the created.

He is sure of our strengths and weaknesses and always remains available to step in and help us if we will only ask. Sometimes prayer is the last thing we do when it should be our first reaction. Praying always seemed to me that I was not being responsible for my actions, and I was taking the easy way out with prayer. Again, independent thinking and self-reliance proved a wrong response.

Now, I better understand that God wants to be involved in every area of our lives, and learning to have a relationship with Him is exactly what He wants from me. To follow His principles is always a choice I have available. Still, to the best of my ability, I must choose to obey His every word to achieve the full victorious results He has made available from His instructions.

We humans also tend to learn from Him then take charge of the following similar situation ourselves. This mistake I have made many times. Each time, as the problem progresses, I realize I've forgotten to call upon Him and apply His Word. My strength is not sufficient to power my way through and reach the godly conclusion I desire. Why? Because this problem is only similar and more is required this time to achieve the victory.

I believe this to be a progressive form of learning that God uses with each problem providing another opportunity to step out in faith and trust Him. This progression strengthens our trust in Him and provides a closer relationship to all He wants to accomplish through us. It's a lifelong schooling process that we each need to learn to grow in faith — continually.

We are each given a measure of faith when our acceptance of Jesus begins. Then, we can grow our faith to enable ourselves to be used in a more significant way to let God exhibit His power through us and be a lamp to unbelievers showing others just what God can do in each life.

Romans 12:3
"Because of the privilege and authority God has given me, I give each of you this warning: Don't think you are better than you really are. Be honest in your evaluation of yourselves, <u>measuring yourselves by the faith God has given us.</u>"

If we don't know our human nature, we will not guard against becoming a partial believer. Believing in God part of the time does not release us into His total care. Gaps in our spiritual application allow holes in our ability to achieve the victory God intends and be a witness to others.

Seeing ourselves clearly in cadence with Scripture is a valuable tool that allows us to see ourselves in the light of the Truth — which is Jesus, our example. His example is our measuring stick in which to compare ourselves (Philippians 2:8). Be careful not to determine your spiritual height by using another person to assess your real stature before God.

When we approach life and its challenges with a partial approach, we reap what we sow (2 Corinthians 9:6). Reaping what we sow is a spiritual truth that always applies and never disappears (Galatians 6:7). Remembering this principle will give you a clue when things may not seem to be happening as we understand Scripture. The Word of God is always true, so any variation reveals loopholes in our application, and the results will yield accordingly.

Living life as a partial believer would be like solving a complicated math problem without using all the required steps to formulate the correct solution. It could be compared to experimenting in a chemistry lab and choosing not to follow all the designated instructions to arrive at the right conclusion. Partially following the instructions would certainly not yield the correct results.

To reap the results of Truth, as explained in Scripture, requires us to apply the designated principles as referenced in the Bible — not just use a selected portion. It requires our full participation and action to make it a reality, as stated. Not just what you think it says, but researching the meaning and then determining how that verse relates to your particular situation to be assured we haven't taken the meaning out of context.

When you read that the Truth will set you free, one must determine to take action and literally apply that truth to your situation. Without your effort in the application, you will discover that true freedom is not fully obtainable. We need to move in a guided, godly direction and do our part in the situation to receive our reward. Scripture has definite principles, and we will yield a godly response only if we fully cooperate with God.

The longer life goes on, the more we need to know to become better conditioned to respond and react as the Lord presents His instructions from Scripture. Leaving out any application in its whole truth will not yield all that God has intended from His instructions. A believer who lives for God on Sunday then spends the remaining days of that week asserting his thinking will undoubtedly experience a limited godly result as far as the Word promises.

If you were to partially play golf for eighteen holes, I wonder how close to par you would come? Maybe you're a person who likes to play horseshoes, and during your game, you haphazardly throw the horseshoe outside the pit? When you're reading a book the next time, stop halfway through and see how well you explain the message or story when you project to others its contents.

Partial participation does not give way to applying yourself fully in accomplishing a task that will bring godly results. The Lord has called us all to fully participate in our faith in Him and step out into the unknown and trust Him. No matter what we see or what we think. We already know from the start that we have a lot to learn, and to operate fully utilizing His help requires us to give our adventure all we can and trust Him for the rest.

Don't be afraid of failure, either. Learning what not to do the next time helps keep us depending on the Lord. Mistakes teach us a great deal in learning how to follow after the voice of God. Our learning process is gradual as we reach out in faith and apply His principles. Don't think you're ever going to stop training to improve your spiritual hearing skills or their intended application.

Should you not be happy with your walk with the Lord, check to see if you are on the right path and that you are following after His Word. A self-examination may be intermittently necessary along your walk to regroup your attention to participate fully to achieve your desired goals.

My personal evaluation caused me to see that I needed to sell out entirely to the Lord and not hold back in any area of my existence because I was fearful it might send me to Africa as a missionary. My silly fear and many other excuses caused me to hesitate in my full cooperation, and the result was a partial walk with the Lord with limited benefits.

Being a partial believer puts you in two completely different elements and persuades you to act one way in the world and a different way at church. When you allow yourself to always fit in with the crowd, you are a hypocrite, which is not a pleasurable or favorable position. We will all experience uncomfortable situations in life, and know they are not uncommon.

May I suggest that you decide before I did and make your choice earlier in life so you can reap all that God intends for you and benefit in having a whole life? An entire life of blessings and prosper beyond your abilities and bask in the presence of the Holy Spirit your entire existence!

It is never too late to sell out completely because God operates in unconditional love (agape). His love is never condemning, always available, and He's eager to help and is fully aware of our shortcomings. His presence is so powerful and so comforting that life completely changes when we allow Him in and fellowship together.

I was recently reading from the Bible and found myself laughing at what I read. What I read was found in the book of John chapter 2, verse 23. It reads:

John 2:22-24

"Because of the miraculous signs Jesus did in Jerusalem at the Passover celebration, many began to trust in him."

"But Jesus didn't trust them, because he knew all about people. No one needed to tell him about human nature, for he knew what was in each person's heart."

When I first read the above of how Jesus expressed what He knew about people and that they weren't trustworthy, I laughed out loud. Our Creator knows exactly about human nature because He knows our hearts. We're a predictable creature and have followed our human nature quite well since our creation. Our pattern of behavior is well documented and very predictable.

We are not trustworthy in our human nature, and the Lord knows it. So, there is no need to try and fool Him. Since He can determine each person's heart — we are revealed whether we think so or not. Our soul, spirit, heart, thinking, and natural instincts are totally exposed, so why believe for a minute we are hidden in any way from the Lord. We not only need to be honest with Him, but we also need to be honest with ourselves!

We might as well be honest before the Lord and pursue the truth of His Word. We should seek His help and allow Him to change us from the inside out. Acting out what we think the Lord wants to see and hear is entirely foolish. We certainly need a mind adjustment if we believe we're that invisible to Him.

Now, realizing the Lord knows us better than we know ourselves, what do you think? We have no excuses before the Lord. And just think, He still loves us anyway and has provided a way to improve our condition. We just need to remember we can't change ourselves, but we can call on Him for His help and cooperate in the transition.

This option we have been offered is life-changing for the better, but we must choose it daily to grasp the beauty of His help and trust Him to bring to completion a work in us only He can do! When Jesus addressed the Pharisees and their skepticism about Him, it revealed much about their belief system. It exposed what their foundation for reasoning was based.

Scripture Reveals the Reason for the Pharisee's Disbelief — Wrong Thinking

John 5:38-47
"And you do not have his message in your hearts, because you do not believe me—the one he sent to you."

"You search the Scriptures because you think they give you eternal life. But the Scriptures point to me! Yet you refuse to come to me to receive this life."

"Your approval means nothing to me, because I know you don't have God's love within you. For I have come to you in my Father's name, and you have rejected me. Yet if others come in their own name, you gladly welcome them. No wonder you can't believe! For you gladly honor each other, but you don't care about the honor that comes from the one who alone is God."

"Yet it isn't I who will accuse you before the Father. Moses will accuse you! Yes, Moses, in whom you put your hopes. If you really believed Moses, you would believe me, because he wrote about me. But since you don't believe what he wrote, how will you believe what I say?"

The Lord knows the heart of man, and it reveals itself in our thinking and actions. Your response to the Truth of God clearly reveals the intent of your heart. Standing on unscriptural beliefs gives others a vivid picture of how we think and believe. God already knows the condition of our hearts if left to ourselves. Maybe it's time we checked out our hearts and turn to the One that can change us.

It doesn't require a physician to do a self-examination. Nor does it call for an x-ray to reveal a severe case of scattered thoughts based on our natural thinking. Once we see ourselves for who we really are and turn to the Lord — we will gather in the healing and spiritual eyesight needed to focus on our future.

Pray with me: Lord, help me see myself in the mirror and visualize what stands before me. A person in need of You to bring me through life and cause me to flourish. Your plan for me is personal, and I want to experience You and bask in Your wisdom and cooperate with Your every word. Thank you, Lord, for providing me with a solution and a future beyond my ability to manage by myself. Amen

Chapter 4

Could Disobedience be My Problem?

Could disobedience be my source for how life is treating me? Could being disobedience be the root cause of my problems in life? Maybe it does have a direct effect, so I should check out my participation in relating to God and determine if there might be a connection. Taking a good look at our choices in life can be very revealing and could answer our present situation or condition.

Looking at ourselves in light of Scripture will provide a truthful and realistic view of where we are and how we are doing from the Lord's perspective. Let's take an example from the Bible that relays a situation that has taken place in real life and the several ramifications that evolved.

I'll reference the story of the Israelites on their journey from slavery in Egypt to the Promised Land, where God's best awaited them. The 400-years of slavery were now ended, and their prayers to God were being answered. He was sending them on an adventure to freedom and being entirely out from under the Egyptian way of life.

The Egyptian way of life was pagan and quite different from what God was releasing them into. The years spent in slavery had given the people of God an environment that was not in line with God's way of living. The breaking away from slavery meant a journey in the transition back to the practices of God and a complete lifestyle change.

The generations leaving had only experienced the pagan way of life. Because of their familiarity with the pagan beliefs, they brought their learned false beliefs with them. The Israeli people still believed in God, but they had many false ideas because of their Egyptian experience in slavery.

When Emperor Pharaoh sent God's people away, he supplied many provisions that would assist them. Pharaoh finally agreed to release the Israelites to end the plagues Moses was sending from God. And, the people of God were undoubtedly not sent away without any belongings and riches on their way through the desert to God's intended destination — the Promised Land. God's plan to free up His people was now taking place in real life as He was answering their prayers.

The journey from Egypt across the desert to the Promised Land was an 11-day journey by foot. Not a great distance but still difficult due to the desert terrain, its desolate location, and severe climate and temperature conditions. The days were sweltering, and the nights were chilling. Due to a large number of people, about 3 million, the difficulties in supporting their many needs would be tremendous.

God took them on this journey to freedom with plans to release them from slavery and enjoy the life He had planned for them. With His help and guidance, they could endure the eleven-day journey and arrive at a destination referred to as 'milk and honey.' The destination was prepared ahead of time and awaited their arrival to enjoy all the benefits God intended.

So, why did it take 40-years to make the distance instead of 11-days? There are multiple reasons, but the main problem was disobedience to follow after the instructions given by Moses from God to the people (Ezekiel 20:13). They were kept informed but followed after some of their old ways learned while enslaved in Egypt. Change can still be difficult even when the destination is desirable.

Imagine resorting to ways contrary to God's instructions and expecting to reap the rewards and benefits of living a better life. To think we can live by our own standards, rather than the Lord's, is a sure way to fall into trouble. God knows this, provided the means to complete the journey and receive all the benefits God had planned for them, including the difficulties they experienced along the journey.

We find ourselves with different circumstances today but remain in bondage should we choose to do our own thing, then expect the Lord to honor our disobedience with favor. This human approach limits our possibilities and keeps us from receiving all that God intends for every believer.

Look at Several Areas that Caused Unnecessary Problems for the Israelites

Idol Worship: Take, for example, how the people acted while Moses was on the mountain for 40-days in fellowship with God and bringing down the Ten Commandments? The people had shifted their worship entirely back to idols rejecting God in their actions. What was the problem?

Rebellion: Consider the people of God (Israelites) and how they complained about everything during the entire relocation. They were not good followers and did not keep their eyes (attention) on the Lord even when they had physical evidence that God existed. With all the lightning, thunder, loud trumpet sounds, and a visual of God's presence was evident as Moses met with God on the mountain. So what did they express?

Ungratefulness: Since they, the people, were far from responsive to God's leading using Moses, they continued on their journey in opposition to almost everything they were instructed. God had planned for them to follow His leadership (through Moses) rather than depend solely on themselves. This journey showed God's people they could rely on Him for everything. It was apparent they needed food and water in the desert. It was obvious their surroundings could not support their needs or assist them on their journey. So what did they display?

Disbelief: It was also obvious the food and water God provided as a means for Him to prove His presence was needed to support their survival. God wanted to increase their faith in Him and build trust and confidence at the same time. Since they declined to view their situation in light of what was going on and move in faith, they chose not to move by faith and accept God's direction. Since they refused to cooperate and fell back into their pagan beliefs, their faith and trust in God did not increase. So, what did they reveal?

Self-Reliance: When the ten spies were sent into the Promised Land to find proof of the plenty awaiting them, what was their response? When the spies returned, eight determined their inability to conquer the inhabitance and chose not to believe that God could be of any significance to help them overtake the residences. They exhibited their lack of faith and decided to depend on their thinking rather than God's reasoning and evaluation. So, choosing to discount God's help equated to?

Stubbornness: This response of independence is rocking chair religion. You can occupy a space, remain in motion but will never get anywhere away from the location you now occupy. You can move or increase your speed (rock faster) but changing the pace accomplishes absolutely nothing. Choosing to remain in our comfort zone leaves no room for faith to take us forward with God's help. Scripture does tell us that faith is what pleases God as we read Hebrews 11:6. A decision not to exercise one's faith counts as a vote to remain where we are and not continue in faith with God. What does this kind of response display?

Unwillingness: Stepping out in faith has its scary moments, but doing so will build our confidence in God and keep us moving closer to the Lord with each step. Remember, fear is from the devil, but being afraid is a normal human reaction to the unknown. A brave person will experience being afraid but will move forward anyway. Each opportunity to experience the Lord will bring an element of being scared, but that condition is shared by all humans. Anytime we step out of our natural human state of comfort, our insecurity will appear. So, we must stop being what?

Faithful Choices: We must learn to depend on the Lord and search for Scripture to find His direction so we can overcome obstacles while using His principles. Putting something we are not sure about into action by faith to resolve a problem will provide the opportunity God offers to each believer to watch Him at work. But, we must choose to step out in faith and not let our instincts decide for us. We must get out of the rocking chair and respond in faith. What is our next step of action?

The Israelites had the Promised Land to look forward to because God said it awaited them. God had already done His part and provided a sample of just what He promised. The remaining effort by the Israelites was to believe Him and move forward in obedience to receive what awaited them. We each have a part to play in achieving the promises of God, and that is to move in faith, believing God above all else. **We can only receive the promises of God by exercising our Faith.**

Responsible Choices: When we hesitate too long or remain stationary waiting for Him to deliver without our cooperation — we wait in vain. Remaining still where we are located will never obtain an active response from God. Our small part in completing and experiencing the final desired outcome remains based on our choice to move in faith toward that goal. It's like having money in the bank awaiting your last withdrawal action to receive it out of an account. If you refuse to go to the bank and withdraw the funds, you will remain broke and wait in vain for the benefits and positive results. Our part is to participate and become involved. That's our part of responsibility in becoming a recipient. We must do our part by making what?

Independence: Those in the large group of Israelites traveling decided not to complete the journey by faith and, as a result, remained trapped in desert conditions as a direct result. The 11-day journey to the Promised Land never arrived. Instead, they traveled continually for 40-years, suffering and experiencing the harsh effects that unbelief yields as their reward. They remained outside the instructions God provided because they determined to stay independent.

God's promise was still valid, but the Israelites did not benefit because they chose to remain, believing they could not overcome the 'giants' in the Promised Land even with God's help. They would not rely on God and viewed the challenge from their perspective only. They couldn't if they relied on their strength; that was true, but if they had followed God's leading by faith, they would have experienced His help to overcome the obstacles that were ahead.

The unbelieving missed completely fulfilling their part of the promise and, therefore, missed the benefits God had planned for them. Their unwillingness to cooperate with God became their action of choice. And their accumulated wrong decisions caused them to reap adverse effects, which resulted in them losing out on all God intended for their future.

1 Corinthians 10:1-11

"I don't want you to forget, dear brothers and sisters, about our ancestors in the wilderness long ago. All of them were guided by a cloud that moved ahead of them, and all of them walked through the sea on dry ground."

"In the cloud and in the sea, all of them were baptized as followers of Moses. All of them ate the same spiritual food, and all of them drank the same spiritual water. For they drank from the spiritual rock that traveled with them, and that rock was Christ."

"Yet God was not pleased with most of them, and their bodies were scattered in the wilderness. These things happened as a warning to us, so that we would not crave evil things as they did, or worship idols as some of them did. As the Scriptures say, 'The people celebrated with feasting and drinking, and they indulged in pagan revelry.'"

"And we must not engage in sexual immorality as some of them did, causing 23,000 of them to die in one day. Nor should we put Christ to the test, as some of them did and then died from snakebites."

"And don't grumble as some of them did, and then were destroyed by the angel of death. These things happened to them as examples for us. They were written down to warn us who live at the end of the age."

What might God have planned for you? Can you back away from your circumstances and focus through the eyes of God and view your current situation in life from His perspective? Sometimes we become so involved in ourselves and our thinking that little room it's left for God. Our self-dependence may leave no room for the things of God. Stepping away and seeing ourselves through another's eyes can be enlightening.

Self-reliance places us alone and at the mercy of chance. The odds are always limited, and our future will be subject to more difficulties relying on ourselves only. Leaving our future life to chance removes the many blessings God intends for our future. He provides the opportunity for each of us but does not negate our free will. Knowing this means you get to choose for yourself. Being given free will is quite a responsibility for each of us. That means we can select the kind of future we desire.

Leaving life to chance means we choose life without God and are willing to receive whatever comes our way. Not choosing to follow after God means we choose to do life alone. In essence, we decide to refuse His help and are willing to subject ourselves to whatever comes our way and tackle the problem independently.

As you view the realities of life, you realize choices are everywhere, and we cannot live a day without making them (choices). Choosing to ignore or refuse His help is your denial to move in a God-designated direction. Once you see that living requires choices, it becomes clear we do not have any choice-less options. We must either choose to follow God or choose not to.

This idea works the same with Scripture and when applying godly principles in your life or choosing not to. Either way, a choice has been made, and your future will directly reflect your selection by its results. The outcome can then be predictable, and your future will give evidence of what choice you made.

Disobedience yields its bad fruit just as obedience will yield godly fruit. What is the fruit, you ask? Glad you asked this question. Fruit is the outcome of a given source — like a tree. If you raise apple trees, you yield apples. If you plant wheat, you will produce wheat. If you sow God's Word, you will reap the blessings associated with this kind of positive action. These blessings are godly fruit.

No matter what you sow, you will reap. Bad behavior has consequences that run a spectrum of possibilities, but not any that are wanted. Good behavior has many benefits that make life easier and eliminate harmful results. You will certainly reap what you sow — no exceptions (Galatians 6:9).

In reading Scripture, I find in Deuteronomy a message meant for us to contemplate our choices and actions. The choices we make will yield the kind of fruit we will produce. The outcome is predictable, giving us examples and providing our opportunity to choose, knowing the results beforehand.

Deuteronomy 30:19, 20
"Today I have given you the choice between life and death, between blessings and curses. Now I call on heaven and earth to witness the choice you make. Oh, that you would choose life, so that you and your descendants might live!"

"You can make this choice by loving the Lord your God, obeying him, and committing yourself firmly to him. This is the key to your life. And if you love and obey the Lord, you will live long in the land the Lord swore to give your ancestors Abraham, Isaac, and Jacob."

Proverbs 2:11
"Wise choices will watch over you. Understanding will keep you safe."

In the Old Testament, God's people were given instructions, and they were cautioned to 'take heart' to what was being said. Because their current conditions were caused by disobedience in the past, there was still hope for their future. So, all was not lost. There was still hope ahead, depending on their choices. It is no different today for us and our current choices (Deuteronomy 30:1-17).

One of the many benefits was that God would change their hearts in the course of their obedience. There is always hope with God and following after His principles. Prosperity follows after an obedient believer (Joshua 1:8). In like manner, the disobedient will suffer the consequences of their choices and reap the path they have chosen to follow (Deuteronomy 27:26).

Success comes with obedience. Success is a benefit you will experience in abundance during your lifetime. The results may be in possessions, or it may be in your labors or all the above. God is not limited. But do remember, He will not give you more than you can bear (handle), and His will is that you grow in a relationship with Him and not turn away at some comfortable point and omit Him from your life.

Your obedience will cause you to become a delight to Him; it will cause His favor to assist you and will ensure His presence always (Psalm 14:5) — especially during the hard times (Jeremiah 7:23). Today we have the Bible and His Word that are readily available. He promises wisdom as we dive into His Word, and the comforter, the Holy Spirit, is always available to teach, direct, empower, comfort, and assist us all along the way (Psalm 25:10).

Following after the Lord your God is a personal choice we each make. Our going after Him with all our might will yield the fruit of blessings, favor, guidance, advice, help, comfort, agape love, godly change, proven instruction results, Eternity with Him, and hope you can't find anywhere else! Our obeying His Word and committing ourselves to follow after Him is our key to a fulfilling life on earth (Deuteronomy 30:20).

Now, the flip side is just the opposite — disobedience will not yield the godly fruit of obedience (Romans 6:16). Scripture provides a snapshot of life in the chosen direction of doing our own thing and wondering what's gone wrong in our lives and why (Ephesians 2:2).

Deuteronomy 30:15,16

"Now listen! Today I am giving you a choice between life and death, between prosperity and disaster. For I command you this day to love the Lord your God and to keep his commands, decrees, and regulations by walking in his ways. If you do this, you will live and multiply, and the Lord your God will bless you and the land (future) you are about to enter and occupy."

The above Scripture is plain talk that we all can understand. I don't want any more difficulty than already exists with just living life. I don't want to complicate the matter, and choosing His help is paramount to me. I've tried life on my own, and it leaves a great deal to be desired. Choosing life with the Lord has caused me to flourish and expand in life to where I'm at peace and enjoying being alive. Even the tuff times, all of it is so much better with the Lord at your side. The comfort the Holy Spirit brings resides within each believer.

Obedience carves our path through life as we follow godly instructions. And, with the Holy Spirit to assist during the journey is also paramount to our yielding to God's intent for our lives. God knows we become weak, make mistakes, and that we need His help (Psalm 119:8). That's why His instructions, when applied, will provide you with guidelines that will reach any level of need that you may require.

Sometimes, even Scripture used once before can be used again in a completely different set of circumstances and work very well. Don't ask me how this works because I don't understand the mysteries God performs. I don't know how He assists us and gets us through in victory in so many different ways.

Let me give you an example of God at work. I'm referring to a story from Scripture that provides a biblical look at a situation from different perspectives. The story about the Prodigal Son gives a viewpoint from the wayward son, the father, and the older brother. We can see three very different perspectives of the same situation as we examine each individual's response. I'm referring to a family story we find in Luke chapter fifteen.

Jesus Gave an Example of a Person Lost and the Value of a Soul

In Luke 15:7, we read:

"In the same way, there is more joy in heaven over one lost sinner who repents and returns to God than over ninety-nine others who are righteous and haven't strayed away!"

God desires that everyone would be saved (John 3:16). He wants all those lost to choose His Son and spend Eternity with Him. The salvation He offers through His Son is made available to everyone. The heart of God that we see today runs consistently throughout all of Scripture.

Take a look at Luke 15:10:

"In the same way, there is joy in the presence of God's angels when even one sinner repents."

Just think, who is in standing in front of God's angels? Jesus! He gets excited over one repenting sinner? He outwardly expresses that joy in heaven whenever this happens! Yes, it brings Him great pleasure when each lost soul accepts His offer of salvation and is saved for eternity.

Now let us Look at the Story of the Lost Son as Described in Luke 15:11-31

Parable of the Lost Son

"*To illustrate the point further, Jesus told them this story: A man had two sons. The younger son told his father, 'I want my share of your estate now before you die.' So his father agreed to divide his wealth between his sons.*"

"*A few days later this younger son packed all his belongings and moved to a distant land, and there he wasted all his money in wild living. About the time his money ran out, a great famine swept over the land, and he began to starve. He persuaded a local farmer to hire him, and the man sent him into his fields to feed the pigs. The young man became so hungry that even the pods he was feeding the pigs looked good to him. But no one gave him anything.*"

"*When he finally came to his senses, he said to himself, 'At home even the hired servants have food enough to spare, and here I am dying of hunger! I will go home to my father and say, Father, I have sinned against both heaven and you, and I am no longer worthy of being called your son. Please take me on as a hired servant.'*"

"*So he returned home to his father. And while he was still a long way off, his father saw him coming. Filled with love and compassion, he ran to his son, embraced him, and kissed him. His son said to him, 'Father, I have sinned against both heaven and you, and I am no longer worthy of being called your son.'*"

"*But his father said to the servants, 'Quick! Bring the finest robe in the house and put it on him. Get a ring for his finger and sandals for his feet. And kill the calf we have been fattening. We must celebrate with a feast, for this son of mine was dead and has now returned to life. He was lost, but now he is found.' So the party began.*"

"*Meanwhile, the older son was in the fields working. When he returned home, he heard music and dancing in the house, and he asked one of*" *the servants what was going on. 'Your brother is back,' he was told, 'and your father has killed the fattened calf. We are celebrating because of his safe return.'"*

"The older brother was angry and wouldn't go in. His father came out and begged him, but he replied, 'All these years I've slaved for you and never once refused to do a single thing you told me to. And in all that time you never gave me even one young goat for a feast with my friends. Yet when this son of yours comes back after squandering your money on prostitutes, you celebrate by killing the fattened calf!'"

"His father said to him, 'Look, dear son, you have always stayed by me, and everything I have is yours. We had to celebrate this happy day. For your brother was dead and has come back to life! He was lost, but now he is found!'"

The son was totally lost (his soul), but now has come to his senses and returned home and is lost no more! His soul has been spared because he chose to seek forgiveness and realized his real destination, having made the wrong choices before. He has discovered the error of his ways and now has accepted the grace and mercy of his father. The son's change of heart reveals his realization **of** error by insisting on doing life his way.

A person on a wrong path will suffer the consequences of his choosing. To realize this error is comforting in that we can still turn from destruction and receive the mercy of a heavenly Father before it's too late. Our perspective of ourselves is vital, and our spiritual situation is critical. Our worth to the heavenly Father is much greater than we sometimes realize. Our soul is of tremendous value to the Lord.

The Desire of God's Heart is: "that no soul should be lost."
Not Even One

John 3:16-21
"For this is how God loved the world: He gave his one and only Son, so that everyone who believes in him will not perish but have eternal life.

God sent his Son into the world not to judge the world, but to save the world through him."

"There is no judgment against anyone who believes in him. But anyone who does not believe in him has already been judged for not believing in God's one and only Son. And the judgment is based on this fact: God's light came into the world, but people loved the darkness more than the light, for their actions were evil."

"All who do evil hate the light and refuse to go near it for fear their sins will be exposed. But those who do what is right come to the light so others can see that they are doing what God wants."

The father's desire was evident, but the older brother had a very different view of the same circumstances. The older son was resentful that, the younger brother did not receive punishment for what he had done. The older brother certainly was not in favor of a celebration!

That was my response when I first read about this story. Why would someone celebrate a fool's return after his sinful choices and rejection of his family? His wandering off to enjoy the desires of his flesh and squandering his half of the inheritance was such a waste.

So now he will return and say he's sorry, and all will be just fine again. I don't think so, 'brother.' You have disrespected our father, you have wasted your inheritance, and now you're going to come back like nothing ever happened. I just don't see your return as a celebration; I see it as a slap in the face, and you should be penalized for your selfish choices and actions and dishonoring our father.

Maybe you feel the same way I did. It would be a normal response in my estimation. Typical as it is, the point being made is far past our natural feelings and human response. How far? God has the right to punish us for our sins. But — He chose to make way for us to be forgiven and return to the Father even though we don't deserve it.

Jesus paid our price for the consequences of our sins and RANSOMED us from the results that follow wrongdoing. God knows we are human and weak and sinful. Our performance is evident throughout the Bible. He is never surprised by our selfish behavior (John 2:25).

I think we sometimes underestimate God's perspective and the depth of His forgiveness. He created us, and He KNOWS just what we're like, how we think our usual mode of operation and our heart without Him in our lives. It's no secret to Him our normal reactions to situations and circumstances. Since He knows our heart and how we think we are predictable. He didn't flood the earth because we were such wonderful human beings. There was a good reason (Genesis 6:1-6).

The older son's perspective in this story reveals he did not understand the message his father was expressing. He missed the whole point. His personal feelings were given charge in his decision-making and caused him to be very short-sighted. Mercy was extended to the younger son because it was required to redeem his soul.

A person's soul is much more valuable to God than our responses based on feelings or limited understanding. The father did not focus on the sin but instead on the change of heart and the son's repentance for his bad choices. So, the lost son coming home was the return of a lost soul, so the father was rejoicing that his son had realized his condition and had decided to return.

God has done just that for our past sins and made a way to save our souls. He has made way for us because He is a merciful God. The choice God made with the cooperation of His Son, Jesus, provided an avenue for us to be ransomed from what we each deserve. Jesus made a way to be redeemed so we, too, can escape what we deserve. He breached the gap between humankind and God. The enmity between God and humanity was forever removed.

This process has been Divinely provided, so we don't get what we deserve being sinners. Because of what Jesus did, we can choose to resolve our dreadful results from sin (eternal damnation) and accept God's provisions of mercy and receive the full benefits God intends for each of us. Our decision to choose to return home, admit our faults, ask for forgiveness, and be welcomed back into God's family is made available — just like the prodigal son returning home.

Like the older brother, those of us need to focus on what is being offered and realize the enormity of what has taken place. Our viewpoint needs to expand beyond ourselves, encompass the whole picture in all situations, and see what is at stake — not allowing our limited natural responses to be based on what we feel and miss the entire purpose.

The provisions God made available can be obtained in our choosing to return to the Father and accept His resolution to our terminal destiny without Him — eternal damnation. Are there circumstances in your life needing to be evaluated and possibly re-examined to consider the purposes of God in it all?

In praying and accepting God's offer of salvation, you have been received back in communication with Him. Your decision to return home will provide you will all the inheritance God has granted to His Son Jesus. Your past will be forgiven, and our Father desires to celebrate your return. Eternity has now been selected, and your physical death on earth will immediately place you present with the Lord in heaven (2 Corinthians 5:1-8).

By accepting the sacrifice God provided, Jesus, our payment for our sins has been satisfied. The desire of God's heart has been granted, and your soul has been ransomed from destruction. Remember, there is joy before God's angels when a soul is salvaged and brought back to Him. Rejoice with Him and join in His Plan for your life while your days on earth continue. That way, you can rejoice with Him both now and all through Eternity.

The Bible tells What is Required of Us to Receive our Right Standing with God

John 5:24-30

"I tell you the truth, those who listen to my message and believe in God who sent me have eternal life. They will never be condemned for their sins, but they have already passed from death into life."

"And I assure you that the time is coming, indeed it's here now, when the dead will hear my voice—the voice of the Son of God. And those who listen will live. The Father has life in himself, and he has granted that same life-giving power to his Son. And he has given him authority to judge everyone because he is the Son of Man."

"Don't be so surprised! Indeed, the time is coming when all the dead in their graves will hear the voice of God's Son, and they will rise again. Those who have done good will rise to experience eternal life, and those who have continued in evil will rise to experience judgment."

"I can do nothing on my own. I judge as God tells me. Therefore, my judgment is just, because I carry out the will of the one who sent me, not my own will."

According to Scripture, it is Good to Follow after Obedience

Nehemiah 9:29

"They did not follow your regulations, by which people will find life if only they obey."

Psalm 111:10

"Fear of the Lord is the foundation of true wisdom. All who obey his commandments will grow in wisdom."

Acts 5:32

"We are witnesses of these things and so is the Holy Spirit, who is given by God to those who obey him."

Luke 6:49

"But anyone who hears and doesn't obey is like a person who builds a house right on the ground, without a foundation. When the floods sweep down against that house, it will collapse into a heap of ruins."

Think about these things!

Chapter 5

How Can Anyone Obey All the Time?

How in the world can humankind always follow after the Lord and be obedient all the time? Is this even humanly possible? No, it isn't — and certainly not in our strength alone, that's for sure. We can't always follow exactly, but we can call upon the Lord for help. And, remember, God does not require exactness anyway. He already knows we can't follow a set of rules flawlessly. We couldn't follow the Ten Commandments He sent, as the Bible clearly reveals.

The Ten Commandments were sent to show us we couldn't live up to God's standards without Him, and they also revealed what He counted as sin. So, how do we view this fact? We first need to realize our inability to follow His standards to the letter and learn His purpose in sending them. The Ten Commandments was God giving us written proof of what is viewed as sinful before Him. These tablets of stone listed what God identified as sin so humankind was made aware and could understand His standards for life.

Each of these commandments provided a 'measuring stick' to visualize and know what was sin according to God. We could then have a perspective of God's instructions. His establishing these standards through Moses is revealed in Exodus chapter 20, so we can learn from this message.

Deuteronomy 5:1

"Moses called all the people of Israel together and said, 'Listen carefully, Israel. Hear the decrees and regulations I am giving you today, so you may prodigal them and obey them!'"

This decree to the people of Israel announced what God wanted from the people. In serving Him, their past, filled with pagan rituals and false gods, needed guidelines since what they had learned while in slavery during their time in Egypt was corrupt. God's written regulations provided the guidance they needed to relate to their pagan ways of thinking and to give them knowledge of how the desires of God would eliminate their continual excuses.

Romans 3:19, 20

"Obviously, the law applies to those to whom it was given, for its purpose is to keep people from having excuses, and to show that the entire world is guilty before God. For no one can ever be made right with God by doing what the law commands. The law simply shows us how sinful we are."

Hebrews 2:2

"For the message God delivered through angels has always stood firm, and every violation of the law and every act of disobedience was punished."

God knowing we can't humanly follow all the commandments, provided a plan to redeem humankind through His Son Jesus. Redemption had been set in place long before the earth was created, as we see in Genesis. A plan where Jesus had agreed to come to earth and die for our sins providing the only sacrifice for sin that could satisfy the Father!

A sacrifice in the Old Testament was only a temporary offering. Because it was only temporary, a sacrifice had to be repeated because a perfect sacrifice had not yet been offered. An acceptable sacrifice had to be spotless and without sin. Since we were born into sin, we could not provide the sacrifice God required to cover our sins. That's why Jesus came to be the perfect sacrifice that would meet God's standards and was able to remove the penalty for sin that was present in the world.

Read the following Bible verses and see for yourself. God's plan for humanity has already taken place, and we have a way to be righteous before God when we accept what Jesus has done for us. God's plan provides each of us an opportunity to present ourselves before God, in Christ, and receive all the benefits God purposed.

Romans 2:4-11

"Don't you see how wonderfully kind, tolerant, and patient God is with you? Does this mean nothing to you? Can't you see that his kindness is intended to turn you from your sin?"

"But because you are stubborn and refuse to turn from your sin, you are storing up terrible punishment for yourself. For a day of anger is coming, when God's righteous judgment will be revealed. He will judge everyone according to what they have done."

"He will give eternal life to those who keep on doing good, seeking after the glory and honor and immortality that God offers."

"But he will pour out his anger and wrath on those who live for themselves, who refuse to obey the truth and instead live lives of wickedness. There will be trouble and calamity for everyone who keeps on doing what is evil—for the Jew first and also for the Gentile."

"But there will be glory and honor and peace from God for all who do good—for the Jew first and also for the Gentile. For God does not show favoritism."

Is Your Heart Right With God?

Romans 2:28, 29

"For you are not a true Jew just because you were born of Jewish parents or because you have gone through the ceremony of circumcision."

"No, a true Jew is one whose heart is right with God. And true circumcision is not merely obeying the letter of the law; rather, it is a change of heart produced by the Spirit. And a person with a changed heart seeks praise from God, not from people."

Christ Took Our Punishment Upon Himself

Romans 3:21-26

"But now God has shown us a way to be made right with him without keeping the *requirements of the law, as was promised in the writings of Moses and the prophets long ago.*"

"<u>We are made right with God by placing our faith in Jesus Christ.</u> And this is true for everyone who believes, no matter who we are."

"For everyone has sinned; we all fall short of God's glorious standard. Yet God, in his grace, freely makes us right in his sight. He did this through Christ Jesus when he freed us from the penalty for our sins."

"For God presented Jesus as the sacrifice for sin. People are made right with God when they believe that Jesus sacrificed his life, shedding his blood. This sacrifice shows that God was being fair when he held back and did not punish those who sinned in times past."

"For he was looking ahead and including them in what he would do in this present time. <u>God did this to demonstrate his righteousness, for he himself is fair and just, and he makes sinners right in his sight when they believe in Jesus.</u>"

The above Scriptures declare the heart of God and His plan for all humanity. All details were ready to be put in place before humanity even came into the picture. God's planning ahead bore great foresight, and that He knew how humankind would act and what they would do in the future.

When I see that God was prepared, it lifts my confidence in Him and eliminates any doubt that He is in charge. Scripture tells us that

74

God is Omnipotent, and just this one example provides us with evidence of His foresight and heart for all humanity.

Scripture provides many examples of God's plan and reveals how He would redeem us from our sinful ways. His plan of redemption allowed our imperfections to be forgiven and put in right standing with God. There was no other way. Even our obedience to the Ten Commandments or our attempt was not possible because of our very human nature and abilities.

Since the Ten Commandments were to show us our sin, they served His purpose well. Through Christ, we can come before God a sinless individual that He accepts (Romans 7:6). Our separation from God can be removed, and our new position in Christ enables us to fellowship with Him once again. This new relationship can make available all that Christ accomplished on the cross — and eliminate the separation from God once and for all.

Our obedience is not evaluated in obeying the Ten Commandments but focuses on accepting Christ and our new position before God. Our ability to never sin again isn't overlooked, but it can always be confessed before God and forgiven in Jesus' name (1 John 1:9).

God's grace and mercy for humankind are presented, and we have the opportunity to be forgiven from the sin nature we were born into and live before the Lord as a new creation, forgiven, pardoned, reestablished in spirit and acceptable to the Father once again (Romans 5:11 & 18).

Our obedience is now in learning to follow after the Holy Spirit God has provided to help us since God has accepted His Son's sacrifice on the cross as our payment in full for sin. We now have access to the Father once we accept Christ as our savior. This opportunity to become the righteousness of God in Christ as a believer has breached the gap sin created between God and man.

This act of faith in the Son of God places us in God's grace, and we are pardoned of the sin we were born into upon our arrival at birth. Our acceptance of Christ puts us in His Son, and when God looks at us, we are now seen from a whole new perspective — we are seen in His Son Jesus (Ephesians 2:1-22).

As we grow and learn about our Creator, God knows we are not knowledgeable of all that is written in the Bible, so our obedience is measured with the idea that we do what we know is right and allow Him to change us during life's journey.

As the Holy Spirit works with a believer, we are prompted to adhere to our convictions of the Word, sermons of significance that speak to our heart, sensing God calling us to respond, spending time with the Lord in prayer and worship. Our putting into action what is expressed to our spirit that was made alive when we accepted Christ.

Maybe you read from Scripture a verse or chapter that caught your attention, and you thought the Lord was talking directly to you. He was! Perhaps you heard a sermon, and you wondered if someone had told the pastor about your situation because it seemed the message was just for you. It was, and you can be assured, God is talking to you — directly!

Or, maybe you keep experiencing the same message coming to mind, and you're wondering why? It is probably the Holy Spirit prompting you to seek an answer from the Bible, talk with another believer, pray about the matter, or put a particular biblical principle into action.

God speaks to us in many different ways to continue giving us opportunities to grasp His guiding our path to a better life. Our obedience to His promptings requires a step in faith and believing Him according to His Word. Since faith is what pleases God, our response determines our obedience to His guidance (Romans 10:17).

When we reject His leading, we are choosing to reject any help from Him. Our rejection to His leading reveals our heart condition and is confirmed by our action of disobedience. Remember — disobedience has its consequences just as obedience does. Our choice of obedience can lead to a better life, and our choice to disobey will yield a much less favorable outcome.

When you look at Scripture in this arena, we can observe that God values our obedience. He values it a great deal because it allows Him to prove out His Word, and it improves our quality of life and the outcome to manifest in our favor. Our actions to follow His principles also glorify the Lord when those around see His character shine through us.

When we look at the Scriptures after Christ came, we find what God wants from us, and that is our obedience. We can now become a living sacrifice offered to the Lord — without dying. Since we are a living sacrifice, we tend to crawl off the altar because it is uncomfortable to remain as we serve him willfully. Nevertheless, our sacrifice of obedience is acceptable and greatly desired by the Lord!

The book of Romans tells us this is our reasonable service, but our placement before the Lord is contrary to our natural likings. Choosing to be a living sacrifice to the Lord is an ongoing decision to accept our role and decide to serve Him. Doing this does require us to die to self which is uncomfortable but necessary to be of service.

Romans 12:1-2
"I beseech you therefore, brethren, by the mercies of God, that ye present your bodies a living sacrifice, holy, acceptable unto God, which is your reasonable service."

"And be not conformed to this world: but be ye transformed by the renewing of your mind, that ye may prove what is that good, and acceptable, and perfect, will of God." (KJV)

Old Testament sacrifices were slain before they were placed on the altar before God. Therefore, we are to offer ourselves and now remain on the altar by choice. We are to stay there by choice without physically dying but to stay there and utilize Christ's death as payment in full for our sins, making it, so we don't have to die. I like this new option much better.

We can now, by faith, accept the sacrifice of Christ and the shedding of His blood, which is acceptable to God, rather than a temporary offering of a dead animal's blood which is temporary. Our acceptance of Christ's sacrifice as payment for our sins completely covers, once and for all, the sin debt we inherited from Adam and Eve.

So, as Scripture relates, being a living sacrifice is our reasonable service to God. Is that correct? It did not sound reasonable to me. I thought when you felt pain; it was a good idea to move out of the current position and remove yourself from the pain. I first thought fleeing provided a safer position and was necessary. That was my reasonable reaction. But, it was wrong.

I had no problem quickly choosing to move and abandon my position on the altar. Then, when I learned more about these verses, I realized that was not what God wanted. I was supposed to be buried with Christ in baptism and to count myself as dead. That was also fun to learn. I've always had difficulty understanding these new ideas once I became a believer.

I certainly needed my mind to be renewed, and I needed an attitude adjustment as well. None of this seemed logical initially, but as I pursued the Lord, my understanding changed. I realized He paid a terrible price for my sins, and I learned and became more grateful as I grew in the Lord.

Our flesh is reluctant to die, so we have to count it as dead, according to Scripture, and allow God to transform us as we submit to Him. We choose, and He does the change on the inside of us. That too seemed strange to me, and it took me years to fully comply, remain on the altar, and be a living sacrifice. It still causes feelings of resistance in me, but I've slowly learned that the future is less painful if you'll let the Lord have His way.

God wanted to remove some flesh, and it is painful to offer it and then have the Lord cut some of it away. This spiritual surgery will not hurt us, even though it does provide some pain, but will prepare us to be made more Christlike in the process and will benefit us greatly in the future! The shorter length of time in being obedient far exceeds the rewards compared to any path I took when I reacted in the flesh.

If we choose to be obedient, our efforts will be rewarded by the Lord. The outcome will strengthen our walk with Him and build our relationship and trust in Him simultaneously. A process that is necessary and beneficial both physically and spiritually. Allowing the Lord to change us to become more Christlike is a process that takes place during our whole lifetime. Thank goodness it doesn't happen all at once!

God is our Father, and He desires what is best for us. The discomfort of offering ourselves as a living sacrifice assures Him we have chosen to follow Him by our own free will. Our freedom to choose is expressed, and He will reward our efforts. The process of growing in the Lord does have growing pains, but should we decide to follow His leadership, our obedience yields a great harvest for Him.

Yes, we have to choose to follow Him daily, and some days can seem harder than others, but the reality of obedience far exceeds any other action because we are dealing with Truth. There is no better way to please the Lord than our obedience to His Word and faith that He will provide the results just like the Bible says. Scripture reveals God's words to each of us directly, personally, and with great wisdom.

When I read the word 'reckon' in Scripture for the first time, I marveled that this word appeared in the Bible. Since I learned to talk as a youth living in Oklahoma, I was told this word was not a correct selection to use in conversation. Then, once I moved to the city, I was taken to speech therapy and taught new words to use and a recommended selection from which to choose. This therapy was to help me replace numerous words from my vocabulary with words more familiar to educated folks.

So, in reading this verse from the Bible, I felt like the Lord was telling me this really isn't a foreign word — but more common than I was taught. Maybe even the Lord had once lived in Oklahoma and understood where I was coming from. Anyway, take a look at the following Bible verse and see for yourself:

Romans 8:18
"For I reckon that the sufferings of this present time are not worthy to be compared with the glory which shall be revealed in us." (NKJV)

This verse was more proof to me that God is personable and knows us very well. We aren't just grouped with other believers but dealt with individually — One on one. We are not lost in the crowd but rather are known by God for who we are, and He relishes this relationship with us.

Knowing God deals with us personally is very exciting and encourages me to move forward. When I read the Bible, I get the feeling sometimes He really is talking just to me. The idea He had the Bible written to help me personally is a wonderful feeling. Sometimes when I read, I understand what I'm reading, and I know the Holy Spirit has taught me more than I could ever have learned on my own. I know the Bible has been written for us all, but sometimes it still feels very special and personal.

Every word in the Bible is His guidelines meant for our benefit. Today, there are so many translations that we can find one that speaks to our spirit like He is standing directly in front of us. His Word is living and offers direction to our spirit that each believer can receive. God's Word is powerful and comes to life in us as we put into action what it tells us (Hebrews 4:12).

The Holy Spirit is our teacher and will quicken the very desire of God's heart and open up a new way of thinking to our minds. His Word will renew our thinking and connect with us by the power of His Holy Spirit. Learning from His Word will allow us to be more easily led by the Holy Spirit and bring into our being the very presence of God our Creator.

As we remain in obedience to Him, we will grow in wisdom and knowledge and be renewed and conformed into the likeness of Christ. This is God's very purpose for each believer and a desirable goal to seek. As we change, it becomes easier to live life as we apply His principles and function as God intends.

So — What is Obedience Anyway?

People view obedience differently, so let's define the several meanings starting with the Merriam-Webster Dictionary. The definition can include any one or all of the following situations giving us a broad spectrum to form our understanding and how best to understand its appropriate meaning and proper application.

1. Obedience can be defined as someone acting in compliance with an order, request, or law or submission to another's authority.

2. Obedience can be an act or instance of obeying, such as children showing obedience to their parents and respect for authority.

3. Obedience can be the state or quality of being obedient: the act or practice of obeying; dutiful or submissive compliance such as military service demands obedience from its members.

4. Obedience in human behavior can be a form of "social influence in which a person yields to explicit instructions or orders from an authority figure."

5. Obedience can be viewed as our willingness to obey the values as presented in the Bible and act out what it recommends.

The Bible Places Great Value on Obedience

1 Samuel 15:22
"What is more pleasing to the Lord: your burnt offerings and sacrifices or your obedience to his voice? Listen! Obedience is better than sacrifice, and submission is better than offering the fat of rams."

The excerpt above is taken from 1st Samuel, which is found in the Old Testament. Sacrifice was a part of offerings to God for the forgiveness of sins. Forgiveness was granted, but it was only temporary. The animal sacrifices were symbolic of Christ to come. This is so amazing because we find this verse written long before Christ had completed His sacrifice on the cross. Do you think God knew He was sending Jesus in the future? Absolutely!

Deuteronomy 11:26-28
"Obey and you will be blessed."

What is the Root Word of Obedience?

To obey is to be obedient, and both words come from the Latin obedire, which means "listen to," but is used to indicate "pay attention to."

What does Disobedient mean in the Bible?

Obedience that God desires stems from love and trust. Jesus said: *"If you love Me, you will obey Me and if you don't love Me, you won't obey Me."*

Disobedience is refusing or neglecting to obey or comply by choice.

God has linked trust in Him, and faith, with obedience. All of God's promises are contingent upon our following His directions. If we obey what He says, He promises that He'll save us, watch over us, take care of us, and provide for our needs.

Why is Obedience so Powerful?

In everyday situations, people obey orders because they want to get rewards. After all, they want to avoid the negative consequences of disobeying because they believe an authority is legitimate.

We receive divine power when we obey God's Word because the Truth of God is released into our lives when we obey His principles.

What is the Nature of True Obedience?

Faithful obedience is when a person's inner being submits their will by faith and behaves according to God's commands. Obedience is the very best way to show that you believe and that you love God.

Is Obedience a Virtue?

Obedience: It is a moral virtue that includes the will to comply with another who has the right to command. Obedience is a virtue that teaches us to be humble. The spirit of obedience helps us to shed our egos and deal with our pride.

Another way that we can show obedience to God is by immersing ourselves in His Word and keeping our thoughts pure. Doing this means spending time reading the Bible and praying daily, avoiding gossip and negative situations, stop watching, reading, or listening to things that don't align with His biblical principles, memorizing Scripture, and the willingness to obey what we learn.

Is it a Sin to Disobey God?

Yes, it is a sin to be disobedient to God's Word. It is arrogantly doing what God says not to do. Then, when God keeps warning us or sends reminders and humans don't pay attention, we rouse His anger, then the drastic consequences of sin emerge; sometimes, it becomes fatal. (Reference Numbers chapter 16 for details.)

Part of being obedient is showing respect to your parents, honoring their ideas about what's best for you, and showing that you value their recommendations. Make sure that you listen when they talk and respond when they ask you to answer. Please don't ignore them or bring shame from your actions.

Obedience, in human behavior, is a form of "social influence in which a person yields to explicit instructions or orders from an authority figure." Obedience is generally distinguished from compliance, behavior influenced by peers, and conformity, intended to match the majority.

Obeying your marriage vows can bring you greater happiness and success in marriage. Disobeying your vows can lead to separation or divorce — or even death.

What Does it Mean to Stand on the Promises of God?

It is the nature of God that makes His promises trustworthy, something sure to stand on. This attribute means that God is unchanging in His character, His will, and promises. Therefore, we can have absolute confidence in God's reliability to make good on His promises because of His unchanging character.

As you can see from the above information, obedience covers many facets of application with enhanced meanings and a broad platform of understanding. A simple way to determine obedience, to me, is to ask myself if I'm acting out in accordance with the Word of God. If I'm following Him to the best of my ability, with the Lord's help, then I'm obedient. If I learn later there are holes in my walk of obedience to the Lord, I purpose to remain open for His guidance and assistance and am willing to receive His correction and follow with a changed response.

I trust the Lord to reveal to me what I need to do next to comply fully. I always keep in mind I'm not perfect and need His help continually. But, when I look back on my life and visualize my progress, I'm happy to see the progression and know I'm better now than I was a year ago. I attempt to remain open to His promptings and to the depth of His Word, realizing the process I'm experiencing is both a blessing and a walk-in grace and mercy He has extended to all believers without exception.

Chapter 6

What Can I Do to Change My Future?

Our choices today definitely affect our future. Each day, each choice, each action will be followed by a direct consequence. That indicates we have the opportunity to make the selection before dealing with our future and experiencing it. It also lets us know we have a great deal in directing our future by what we do and say today.

If we choose to avoid making choices, then we have opted to take our chances. Taking our chances allows whatever happens in our future to be determined by someone or something other than ourselves. This approach is quite dangerous and will leave you susceptible to many difficulties in the days ahead. The rewards of chance are pretty limited and have proven out over many years of application with inferior results.

Yes, we each have circumstances that we did not choose, but we must deal with because of our environment, location, and everything else involved. That is not the area that I'm talking about. I'm talking about what you choose as your next move to improve your current life conditions from a biblical standpoint.

Are you waiting to become obedient at some future point? Don't you want to reap in your future the things of God? Are you willing to follow the directions recommended in the Bible no matter what? Are you ready to make a decision and stick with it and see it through?

We each have a given environment in which we were born. This environment, of course, was not of our choosing, but it is where we begin life. As we grow into adulthood and become more independent, we must make godly choices to improve and change from where we started. Our biblical choices will operate in any environment and produce a crop based on the seed we sow.

For example, if we sow grass seeds in our yard, we expect to see the grass grow from these seeds and produce a green grassed yard. If we were to sow dandelion seed, we would expect to see a yard covered with green pods making a yellow bloom that will yield a seed pod that can be blown by the wind and seed the whole area for the next season.

The kind of seed we sow is what will be produced. Growing up on a wheat farm in Oklahoma gave me a visual picture of sowing seed. The soil preparation, planting of these seeds in September, waiting for growth during the winter. Then in the spring, growing into a stalk yielding a head of wheat with many grains of wheat being produced. Then, by June, a golden crop of ripened wheat ready to be harvested and sold by the bushel. It took about a bushel of grain per acre of seed when planting and yielded about 30 bushels per acre at harvest time (Mark 4:8).

The point is that what was sown was reproduced when the seed had completed its growth cycle. And it produced a crop that multiplied when harvested. This process is similar to sowing seeds of Scripture given to us from the Bible. As God's Word provides examples, our sowing good seeds can be multiplied through us as we let Him reproduce them in our lives.

Indeed, there will be seasons, storms, wind, sunshine, rain, and circumstances that may threaten what God is producing in us during this time, so don't find this unusual. But, you can be certain a multiplied crop will be yielded when we complete the harvest season, trusting He will produce godly results in our lives.

Maybe you thought your family was a mess, and that wasn't fair. You may have a friend that seems to have had the ideal family setting and that if you could have been born in a family like theirs, your life would be much better. All that may be true, but you have to deal with where you are — not from where they were.

You could probably share numerous events about your life that weren't fair. Had these events not taken place, you could have easily been in a better position and would not have hampered you getting ahead sooner? Most of us relate to our life history and can see where it could have been better, but that is the past, and we are in the present and planning for the future. Today, of course, is now, but tomorrow is the future — right?

So let's get started today and make choices that will affect our tomorrow and be in our favor. That means a new beginning and hope for what lies ahead. It means we can be a positive part of our future, unlike our past. Looking ahead accompanied by scriptural planning is necessary to move forward and reap a good crop.

Trying to move forward while we're looking back the whole time will become more than a pain in the neck. It will cause our future to be based on past difficulties, feelings, and emotions, limiting positive change or healthy growth. The things in our past causing problems are called baggage, and the Lord did not design us to carry this load.

Carrying this baggage will likely cause your whole life to remain the same and change nothing for the better in your future. And, if your future is left to chance — chances are you won't like it any better than the past. If we want to move forward and include our dreams and hopes, we must obtain the Truth of where we are now and what is necessary to enhance our future. Knowing this is why biblical principles and their application are so critical.

If we have the mindset that adjusting our present conditions will only be more troublesome, we have learned to accept the way things are currently with no hope for the future. With our human nature, we have the strange ability to stay in the boiling pot rather than escape, with a little effort, to a better location in life.

This scenario seems to be a general rule when it comes to human reactions to change and is commonly the nature we choose rather than shake up the boiling broth because it may make things worse. We should consider this point during our selections to closely determine the best direction to follow through prayer.

A baby is aware that they need a diaper changed and usually let us know should we not be paying attention to their current discomfort. We need to consider our present condition and determine if a change is required to avoid future discomfort and irritation. Since a baby can quickly determine the need for change, why can't we assess our source of discomfort and irritation and be open to a change?

Our grownup diaper might have needed to be changed long ago. However, we still have the opportunity to shed many problems in our lives with a chance to renew our thinking. And with the application of godly principles available to each of us, we can grow in the Lord. Like I said before, maybe a self-examination is needed in light of Scripture to determine if a change would lay out a better plan for your future than the plan you are now using?

The unwanted items in your life need to be identified, and the Lord is the one who can instill what needs to be changed in you. The necessary condition is that you will choose to let the Lord intervene so He can begin the required adjustments. Your cooperation and willingness are essential to start this process. Allowing the Lord to fill in where change will benefit you and removing the unwanted circumstances now standing in the way can lead you to a better life.

Knowing only godly change will be lasting is critical to understand and accept. The needed changes we all require only God can make. Yes, humankind can adjust a few characteristics about themselves, but they usually fall short in the long run. Character building needs God's input to achieve lasting results.

Your current path is documented by the results you are now experiencing. To surpass your current level of operation, we must call for God's help and apply His scriptural principles. This procedure requires us to endure the necessary needed adjustments in our selection and choices. It requires a change that will only occur as we yield to Scripture and cooperate with a willing spirit. The change will require your flesh to succumb to the Spirit of God. A choice you will need to implement if you want to move forward.

Expect and adjust to the discomfort this obedience will bring to your flesh. The temporary discomfort will soon be minimized with each choice to allow the Lord to work. And, the results that follow will far exceed the temporary discomfort you've suffered (Hebrews 5:8). The slight pain to achieve godly results is well worth any yielding to the Holy Spirit of God working in you.

Growing pains in the spiritual realm are similar to the growing pains we receive naturally and will occur. Feeding your spirit God's Word will provide the nourishment needed to progress in your walk with the Lord. An accomplishment we experience as we work with the Lord in continued cooperation. Growing in the exchanged life will materialize through each learning level (Romans 8:18).

Reaping the benefits of obedience is very rewarding. As godly results begin to replace unwanted crops, we find encouragement to what continued growth in the Lord will produce. Harvest season will arrive and is a time to celebrate the best-achieved crop of multiplied seed. Enjoying your changed life and reaping the rewards that follow are definite signs of what the Lord has in store for you. There is no limit or end during our lifetime of what the Lord will accomplish in us as we stay on track following after His leading obediently.

As we continue to grow, the choices we make become a reality. Our previous worldly fundamental thinking starts changing and causes us to lean in the direction we now believe. This process changes our thinking and renews our minds to better understand and benefit from the Lord. This process is ever-increasing and always available to every believer. Some choices are better than others, but each will directly impact our future because there are consequences for every choice (Galatians 6:9).

This needed change is when the Bible becomes a way of life. If our choices come from the Truth expressed in God's Word, we can obtain a better end result. I have seen people who practice godly principles but do not accredit the Bible for any of the positive results. They tell me they were raised that way and followed the guidance they learned from their parents and family. Some tell me the reason is that they were smart enough to do the right thing on their own. In addition, they knew what not to do because they witnessed bad results from watching others make bad choices and suffer the consequences.

That is all well and good, but I'm talking about a greater depth to be found in Scripture as we become a believer and apply godly principles in every choice we make. That is, to the best of your understanding, according to the Word of God. Principles from Scripture are divine seeds that will produce a good harvest no matter who uses them.

As believers, we also learn that following Godly principles are critical in every decision and very beneficial. The Bible tells us that God's Word stands firm and will always come to pass (Mathew 4:4; Psalm 119:89). A foundation based on divine wisdom is a solid, repetitive, God ordained structure of building blocks we can rest assured our future will yield the intended results.

I've listened to folks as they tell me they did not plan for retirement or their future. As I listened, I learned they didn't want to change how they viewed money or handled it. And they weren't willing to change what was necessary to accomplish a realistic goal. But, because they saw that I had good results in my life, they wanted me to help them.

My answer was sobering to them because I could not scripturally fix their future at this late stage in their lives. They had waited too long and still weren't open to any changes that would reap better results. Even those necessary changes to partially reach their goal were rejected because they did not want to initiate any changes to their present conditions.

It troubled me to think they thought a quick fix from Scripture would erase their neglect from their past. They were believers, but for some reason, had not dealt with money in their past scripturally and waited until the end of their lives to maybe consider it for the first time. As a result, all of their retirement had been left to chance. Kind of like hoping for the best, but without any participation or plan to help make it happen.

I soon learned the preparation for retirement was avoided because they wanted to live life the way they did with no regard for the future. They lived for the moment; then, they assumed they could call for a biblical lifesaver after they had gone down the path they chose and drowned in the lifestyle of their past choices. The lousy seed they had sown would soon produce a harvest they did not want to experience.

God is definitely a lifesaver, but this form of neglect on their part was a choice, and even though it was long and slow in happening, they had left their retirement to chance. The 'chance' results proved to be very sorrowful and left them doubting their faith in God. Because their choices were made without God involved from the beginning, they weren't getting the end results they had hoped. God was not allowed to help them because they never called and asked for His help until the very end of their lives.

This scenario repeats itself over and over as I listen to people tell me their life stories. Some have started earlier and have found the Lord can do miracles, and they benefited greatly. So, questions come to the surface as we reflect on our past choices. How are you planning your future, and what do you expect to find? Do you think some unexpected event will supplement your neglect and save you from failure?

Does leaving your future to chance seem like a good way to produce any godly results?

The story about the non-planning couple is evident, but in reality, they were responsible for making their choices all through life and could have avoided the bleak retirement they reaped. How do we plan ahead and ensure our future is not doomed before we even get there? Yes, there will be mistakes, and there will be streaks of sadness no matter what on our journey. But leaving everything to chance and living for the moment is certainly not the best choice for anyone.

I have a suggestion, and this is not advice, but rather a look from my viewpoint as one that has reached retirement and is enjoying the fruit of what God has accomplished in my life the last seventy-some years. It was not me making anything happen supernaturally in the stock market because I'm so smart or talented. It was because I realized I could achieve much more by calling upon the Lord and utilizing His principles to help me. I learned that what He says will come to pass! That was my choice through life, and I tried to make choices based on Scripture at every turn.

Isaiah 55:11
"It is the same with my word. I send it out, and it always produces fruit. It will accomplish all I want it to, and it will prosper everywhere I send it."

First, I found that getting to know the Lord was a decision to accept His Son Jesus, commit my life to Him, and discipline myself to practice the principles spoken in the Word of God. This change to my approach to living involved many mistakes on my part, but the overall process was very successful and rewarding. I started sowing good seed, and God bless my obedience to Him.

There were times I thought His ideas were just plain stupid, but I moved forward and did what He said anyway. I went at His principles slowly because I was somewhat fearful they might not work. I was surprised when I found myself in a new position with my circumstances. It proved out that when God's Word was applied, it yielded great results that were just like He said. I found this exciting, so I would continue to grow in faith, trust Him more, struggle, and plan and progressively succeed through each stage in my growth.

It amazed me how the Bible could have been any help since life is so different today. There is undoubtedly a tremendous amount of His wisdom available to conquer and overpower obstacles that fall in our path to life's end. The road ahead is not always clearly visible, but His guidance down a dark path is enlightening. Having faith in our next step, when obeying Him, is the right direction and is comforting and builds our confidence.

As I grew and applied God's principles, read the Word, fellow-shipped with other believers, I found victory over numerous snags, peace beyond my wildest dreams, and a relationship with our God that I never thought was possible. My lifetime of practicing the principles from the Word of God has been ever increasing over the years. And always spectacular in the unfolding and the fruit of God they produce.

Why I'm writing books now even though I didn't do very well in speech therapy during my youth and still don't always know what word is best to use to get my point across, I still struggle with a few words, but that doesn't stop my writing — it just slows the process down a little. Nevertheless, this is my fourth book, and I look forward to seeing what's next. My future has opened up new opportunities to share what God has done in my life!

In viewing the overall picture, I find the wisdom of God is provided to each believer according to the Bible. Remember, our endeavor to find His answer starts with our new beginning in Christ. In reading God's Word, a believer soon realizes His vision is in print. It provides written evidence that everyone who applies its many different applications to our living life is enormously beneficial. Its wisdom has never failed me yet, and I've been practicing for many years.

When I thought maybe it wasn't working in application, I learned God's timing was quite different from mine. I certainly believe God acts promptly in response to our prayers, but timing is critical. And, there are still a few answers that took a more extended amount of time to answer because of the people involved. Circumstances and reactions that were necessary to benefit everyone involved must be included.

God likes to answer prayers in line with His perfect will and what is in our best interest. (See about King Hezekiah in chapter 7.) God allowed King Hezekiah to have his wish, and it brought very negative results in the future leadership of Israel. It has proven out that when asking Him in prayer, I think it is good practice to seek only what is in our best interest and to trust Him for the best overall results. That, of course, includes His answer no sometimes.

I Have Grown to Believe

I now choose to wait, knowing His timing will always be perfect. I also don't want Him to answer a prayer of mine that will not be in His or my best interest. God has set life up to save us from the sin in which we were born. He has provided an instruction book with helpful principles and wisdom that apply beyond our understanding. He has given instructions that when applied with change our thinking and renew our mind from our natural viewpoint. And because He wants to bless us at every opportunity as we act out in obedience to His instructions.

If put in His realm of operation, our future provides us with a prosperous future full of the good things in life that He intends for us to experience. Then, when this life is over, He has a plan for eternity that includes every believer enjoying the endless beauty of Heaven — and His Presence forever (Jeremiah 29:11).

So, we're back to choices once again. Now is the first day of the rest of your life — heard that before? Well, it's true. Unless you're 120 years old, you can start today and still find a bright remaining future with an excellent eternal retirement package. Starting too late may spoil your end-of-life financial problems and numerous blessings, but the change may resolve many obstacles that will appear and give you a better life as you journey toward eternity.

The choice is solely yours. No one else can make this decision for you. God is anxiously waiting for you to select Him and let Him help guide you into the unknown. He has a plan for your life because you weren't placed here on earth by mistake. You were selected by Him, woven together in your mother's womb, and chosen for such a time as this (Psalm 139:15).

The beginning anew is left to your free will and choosing for yourself. Why? Because God wants you involved with Him to help you take the best path possible. Won't you invite Him into your existence and be willing to learn and grow in His wisdom as He helps direct your journey? You are only one prayer away to start a new beginning. (See the end of chapter 2.)

Check out the following story about Joseph from the Bible regarding his life and the many problems he faced on his journey to be used by the Lord. His path included obstacles most people never face, yet because he was faithful to God, he proceeded continually forward even when put in places never thought or seemed likely or fair.

In Genesis chapters 37, 39-50, and learn about Joseph and his loving family. Joseph was the son of Rachel and was favored by his father Jacob above all the other children. Scripture tells us Jacob favored Joseph because he was born of his wife Rachael when he was old. This favoritism brought hatred from his half-brothers, and that hatred put Joseph in grave danger and challenging situations.

So much danger that it prompted his brothers to sell Joseph into slavery rather than kill him, which placed him in numerous severe situations with grave consequences. The key to success was that Joseph took every opportunity always to exhibit his faith in God. Joseph had choices to make, and he chose to depend on the Lord no matter what he faced, always looking to the future with hope.

Some of Joseph's Major Hardships were:

- Totally rejected by his half-brothers.

- Sold into slavery because of their jealousy and hatred for him.
- Jailed for 13-years because of a false accusation from Potiphar's wife.

In all these different situations, Joseph was innocent but remained faithful to God. He did not falter in his actions and repeatedly found favor from the Lord in every location. How is this possible? He even found favor in a place of detention. In each situation, Joseph was found to have a good attitude, was an unfailing trusted worker, diligent in his duties and faith, and superior in his ability to perform intelligently. He could interpret dreams with accuracy as God directed him.

This determination to follow after God placed Joseph in great favor in the eyes of Pharaoh, the Egyptian king. Pharaoh had two dreams from the Lord. Both were dreams from God to Pharaoh warning of what was coming in the future. When Joseph was called to interpret Pharaoh's two dreams, much was revealed.

The interpretation forecasted seven years of great prosperity followed by seven years of famine throughout the land of Egypt and surrounding areas. It would require good resourceful planning, adequate preparation and expanded storage locations, with intense supervision to tackle what lay ahead to avoid starvation.

Joseph presented what all was needed to be prepared in the presence of Pharaoh and his officials. His interpretation of the two dreams and strategy to resolve was well received. His solution provided what was necessary to survive during this 14-year event. This plan would allow Egypt to survive the severe famine foretold that was to take place in Egypt and throughout the surrounding region.

As a result of Joseph's interpretation of Pharaoh's two dreams plus a proposed detailed solution, he was put in charge to carry out the details and serve the Pharaoh as second in command over Egypt. Moving from a prison to a palace was quite a change, but since Joseph was serving God the whole time, he was well prepared for what God had in store.

His new high-ranking position placed him exactly where God needed him to save his whole family back in Canaan. Joseph's father Jacob and family resided in Canaan, where the famine also placed them in a severe food shortage condition. And, because Joseph's family was fearful of starving, they needed to go to Egypt to purchase food. This chain of events would bring Joseph's family back together, but it was not exactly a typical family reunion.

Unbeknown to the family of Jacob and his half-brothers, Joseph now ruled in Egypt and would be the very person they would have to contact to purchase the much-needed food. Their encounter with Joseph was interesting because they did not recognize their brother, but he recognized them.

Joseph decided to determine the character of his brothers, so he tested them to see how they would respond. Joseph placed money in the brother's purchased grain bags, which was not discovered until later. The presence of this money could indicate to outsiders the money was stolen while they were in Egypt.

On his family's next trip back to Egypt, Joseph greeted them and invited them to his palace for a meal. Once the meal ended and Joseph's family was ready to leave, Joseph instructed his palace manager to fill their sacks full of food but place their money in the bags and put Joseph's silver cup into one of the sacks before their departure.

This second adventure by Joseph involved another opportunity for his brothers to rise above the situation presented to them by the palace manager. This again involved a test of their honesty and a means to bring Benjamin, his younger brother, back to Egypt, as well as his father Jacob, when they returned the next time.

At this juncture, Joseph revealed to his brothers who he was. He was their brother Joseph whom they had sold into slavery many years before. Their dastardly deed had resurfaced, and Joseph shared with them how God had orchestrated the entire circumstances using Joseph to save their family during this time of drought and severe famine they were now experiencing.

Now was two years into the seven-year famine when this all became known to everyone involved. Joseph told his brothers to bring their father Jacob back to Egypt from Canaan, and they could dwell in the Goshen region close to him. They could survive the famine and live without fear of starvation in a new location, ensuring their survival during the severe conditions.

God had provided the opportunity for Joseph to bring his family out of Canaan into the region of Goshen near him. His purpose was to save them all from starvation during this terrible time of famine throughout the land. This chain of events now brought healing to all due to Joseph's forgiveness and faithfulness, trusting God through all his challenging circumstances (Psalm 105:17-23).

We each have a story involving our years of living that might surpass even what Joseph went through. No matter the circumstances, we have the same opportunity to remain faithful to God and trust Him to complete in us what our purpose in life involves. Don't think for a moment you don't have a purpose when God is allowed to guide us — no matter what it may seem like at the time.

Did your past bring rejection, hurt by family members, the harm that God turned into a purpose, and very uncomfortable situations — but with God's help turned out well? Our choosing to follow after the Lord is no different now than it was for Joseph. It indeed reveals that our obedience to the Lord will always materialize into God's desired outcome! Our determination to keep our eyes on the Lord and follow after Him will certainly bring purpose and fulfillment.

Joseph spent 13-years in prison because of false accusations, his continued good attitude to trust God no matter what, and his constant focus on God kept him continually headed in the right direction. That was his pursuit during all the adverse circumstances. He didn't let himself become angry with God over the unfairness that continued to come his direction. He hung in there no matter the obstacles that came to his attention, trusting in God by faith the whole time.

Looking back over his life from a distance, we can determine that the Lord used each circumstance to continually change Joseph into the man he needed him to become. The continued attitude of Joseph placed him in God's hands, and his willingness allowed the necessary changes to occur. The timing of God was perfect to incorporate all involved. Each of us has this very same opportunity today.

Our choices in life and our willingness to follow after the Lord will give Him the same opportunity He needs to change us into the godly character required to be beneficial to God in our future. Being transformed is so contrary to our natural desires it will cause temporary difficulties, but the results are well worth the minor struggles (1 Peter 1:14).

Had Joseph allowed himself to become bitter and resentful toward God, he would have missed the needed changes in his character. It would have eliminated his opportunity to follow God's desired path for his life. Had Joseph refused to accept and trust in God, he would never have been capable of becoming mighty before the Lord. His changed character gave him the ability to perform the duties God needed to bring blessings to his family and himself.

None of the situations he encountered would Joseph have chosen, but since he pursued his future in faith, he received his reward from God. As Joseph made choices to serve God, he forgave his brothers, rose to become second in command in Egypt, saved his family from starvation, and was reunited with his father Jacob and fulfilled God's very purpose for all their lives.

In all of the severe famine that came, Joseph also saved the lives of many Egyptian people and made arrangements to work with them, so food was available to feed their families. The wisdom God gave Joseph was utilized by him as directed, which fulfilled God's plan for the nation of Israel, and they prospered and were very fruitful all during this difficult time.

Joseph's father Jacob lived seventeen years after arriving in Egypt, where he lived out his life. The large picture of time during this problematic famine became a blessing to all involved. The Egyptians and Israelites both survived the famine successfully. This event is a witness to us today how God continues to work in the life of His people.

The Bible is full of stories of faithful servants, which reveal that God changes men because they choose to follow Him no matter their circumstances. Their obedience took them beyond themselves and their capabilities to experience a newness in life. Our God-given spirit of free will continues and allows each of us to choose our path in life. Each believer in God has the same opportunities during their lives to decide for themselves what direction they desire.

Our God is eager for us to follow after Him and choose the direction He has planned for us individually. None of us are able on our own to accomplish God's plan for our lives. But, with His help, the road to a fulfilled life is available. Of course, our lives are each different, but overall we are much the same. As we each complete our purpose on earth, God's Plan is fulfilled one person at a time.

Our circumstances occur in different environments, families, difficulties, personalities, physical size, intelligence, abilities, thinking, experiences, locations, etc. Nevertheless, we each have a starting point to take what we have, choose what we want to do in life, and flex our free will. This choice will lay out our future and utilize His help to fulfill our very purpose on earth.

Yes, there will be resistance all along the way, but we can choose the path of faith or choose the path without God. There is a great responsibility given to each of us, and there are no excuses when it comes to choosing. We have the freedom to choose what we desire with clear indications from the Lord what the consequences for each will produce (Deuteronomy chapter 28).

Joseph could have reflected on his past circumstances and made excuses for himself. He did not have a life without opposing forces coming against him — almost continually. Nevertheless, Joseph chose to follow after God by faith, and his relentless pursuit relied entirely on God to construct his future no matter the circumstances. It was a choice to serve God — but he could have chosen not to.

Joseph used his free will to choose, and the story of his life yielded the fruit of his faithfulness to God. He didn't have God's written word to follow as we do but relied on his faith to get him through. And the results were tremendously favorable and glorified the Lord.

Joseph fulfilled his destiny and purpose in life because he chose wisely. This Old Testament person set an excellent example for us to consider regarding our own lives. Do you want to fulfill your purpose in life by yourself, or would you like the hand of God guiding you along the way?

Look at the evidence in Scripture from the results of being obedient. Joseph remained in obedience by choice even though he had no fellowship with believers once he was sold into slavery. His foundation was established early in life, and even with the difficulties, he continued in the Lord. This unwavering faithfulness had much resistance, but Joseph continued to choose God anyway.

His prison ministry came from his willingness to follow after his beliefs no matter the circumstances. His obedience provided him with the favor of his jailers and fellow prisoners. The baker and chef that joined him in jail came directly from Pharaoh's staff. Joseph's ability to interpret their dreams with followed proof provided him a chance to exhibit his divine gift.

Even though his favor with Pharaoh was not immediate, the chance to interpret the two dreams eventually came. Pharaoh enabled Joseph to utilize his gifting that opened the door for his release and promotion to second in command. Thirteen years is a very long time to be imprisoned unfairly with no relief in sight. His task, when completed, yielded great favor and success because the Lord was with him.

Just think — Joseph continued in faith, not knowing what lay ahead. Blind faith is very pleasing to God and reveals to Him much about a person's character. Believing for the best and still living in the not-so-good environment was more than being optimistic. It was faith — believing in God even though we physically see no evidence (Hebrews 11:1).

It certainly isn't too late for you. If you're breathing, your opportunity is still available. I waited a long time to get serious about my relationship with the Lord. I was aware of His presence as a child, but I did not pursue Him with all of me. I would leave out certain areas I did not want to deal with to do what I wanted instead. There was obviously ignorance, but primarily resistance and a lack of willingness to commit all the way.

I was afraid to sell out entirely because I did not want to be called somewhere I might be uncomfortable. I allowed my fleshly desires and fear of the unknown to keep me just off track enough to remain making choices that weren't entirely on track. Getting older has taught me to rush forward and resist my natural inclinations and open those areas of resistance to the Lord. The results have been very pleasing to me, and I could have made that choice years earlier but resisted instead.

I thought I could guess what might occur and was fearful I would not like the new location. My fears blocked the path God had for me and limited what usefulness I could have been to the Lord. Our natural thinking does need to be renewed in the Word of God so we can move on past the captivity of our limited thinking.

As I look back from today, I'm so grateful I followed the Lord and turned Him loose in my life. The blessings that have followed have enriched my whole being, and I now embrace His presence to a level I did not know existed. My growth depended on my surrendering all rather than operating at a level of fear that deferred what He had in store for me.

The God we serve as a believer is quite capable of leading us into a profoundly active life as we fellowship with Him. I haven't arrived at the level He desires for me yet, but I'm moving in a much better direction now with renewed hope for the future. Our forgiving God is waiting on each of us to choose the path He has prepared. It isn't too late — not with God!

Chapter 7

Can My Life and Purpose Still be of God?

Yes, your life with the Lord starts the minute you accept Him into your heart. This acceptance is so simple that we think there must be more to this than the Bible describes. As explained in 1 Corinthians to follow, the opportunity God provides is looked upon by the world as foolishness.

1 Corinthians 1:18-23

"The message of the cross is foolish to those who are headed for destruction! But we who are being saved know it is the very power of God. As the Scriptures say, 'I will destroy the wisdom of the wise and discard the intelligence of the intelligent.'"

"So where does this leave the philosophers, the scholars, and the world's brilliant debaters? God has made the wisdom of this world look foolish. Since God in his wisdom saw to it that the world would never know him through human wisdom, he has used our foolish preaching to save those who believe."

"It is foolish to the Jews, who ask for signs from heaven. And it is foolish to the Greeks, who seek human wisdom. So when we preach that Christ was crucified, the Jews are offended and the Gentiles say it's all nonsense."

No, God has provided a way that takes us into His kingdom as we confess our sins before Him and receive Jesus into our hearts. This acceptance releases the Holy Spirit of God to dwell inside each believer and provides the help we need to move forward with Him.

Romans 10:19-22
"Obviously, the law applies to those to whom it was given, for its purpose is to keep people from having excuses, and to show that the entire world is guilty before God."

"For no one can ever be made right with God by doing what the law commands. The law simply shows us how sinful we are."

How Can This Be? Because — Christ Took Our Punishment

"But now God has shown us a way to be made right with him (God) without keeping the requirements of the law, as was promised in the writings of Moses and the prophets long ago."

"We are made right with God by placing our faith in Jesus Christ. And this is true for everyone who believes, no matter who we are."

Scripture Tells What We Must Do to Receive Salvation

Check out this question asked by the jailer in the book of Acts. Paul and Silas prayed with their jailer in response to his request. So, he and his whole family were saved during that one encounter and rejoiced to the Lord for their salvation.

Acts 16:29-34
"The jailer called for lights and ran to the dungeon and fell down trembling before Paul and Silas. Then he brought them out and asked, 'Sirs, what must I do to be saved?'"

"They replied, 'Believe in the Lord Jesus and you will be saved, along with everyone in your household.' And they shared the word of the Lord with him and with all who lived in his household."

"Even at that hour of the night, the jailer cared for them and washed their wounds. Then he and everyone in his household were immediately baptized. He brought them into his house and set a meal before them, and he and his entire household rejoiced because they all believed in God."

The Old Way and the New Way in Comparison

2 Corinthians 3:7-18

"The old way, with laws etched in stone, led to death, though it began with such glory that the people of Israel could not bear to look at Moses' face. For his face shone with the glory of God, even though the brightness was already fading away."

"Shouldn't we expect far greater glory under the new way, now that the Holy Spirit is giving life?"

"If the old way, which brings condemnation, was glorious, how much more glorious is the new way, which makes us right with God! "

"In fact, that first glory was not glorious at all compared with the overwhelming glory of the new way."

"So if the old way, which has been replaced, was glorious, how much more glorious is the new, which remains forever! Since this new way gives us such confidence, we can be very bold."

"We are not like Moses, who put a veil over his face so the people of Israel would not see the glory, even though it was destined to fade away."

"But the people's minds were hardened, and to this day whenever the old covenant is being read, the same veil covers their minds so they cannot understand the truth. And <u>this veil can be removed only by believing in Christ</u>."

"Yes, even today when they read Moses' writings, their hearts are covered with that veil, and they do not understand. <u>But whenever someone turns to the Lord, the veil is taken away</u>."

"For the Lord is the Spirit, and wherever the Spirit of the Lord is, there is freedom. So all of us who have had that veil removed can see and reflect the glory of the Lord. And the Lord—who is the Spirit—makes us more and more like him as we are changed into his glorious image."

The Old Way required us to follow the Ten Commandments in every detail. Not one rule could be broken, or else we were guilty and remained apart from fellowship with God. If we lied, we were as guilty as one who murdered someone. And, since we were human, this following every detail was impossible. Humans don't have the ability on their own to react correctly all the time and be sinless.

God knew we could not live by a set of rules to become sinless. These rules did reveal what was not acceptable to God and was considered a sin. In Him writing them on stone, He spelled out His standards and what it would take to fellowship with Him — a Holy God completely separate from all sin! And, must remain separate to remain Holy!

So, what was the solution? Jesus had agreed with God before the earth was created that He would sacrifice Himself in our place to meet the requirements of God to be forgiven of sin committed in the Garden of Eden. This discussion all took place in Genesis 1:26. A godly solution was already in the works before it was needed.

Then, when the time was right, God sent his Son Jesus, a perfect, sinless sacrifice, into the world to take away (permanently remove) the sin of the world (2 Corinthians 5:21). Jesus became human and lived out His 33 plus years being in the form of a human, born through a virgin woman, but remained a member of the Trinity — Divine.

He was both human and God at the same time. Jesus was God in a fleshly form that could take our place under the Old Way, meet its requirements because He was sinless, and create a New Way to resolve the separation sin caused that humanity had created with God. This New Way resolved the sin issue and breached the gap sin created with God.

It Still Works the Same Today

Romans 3:23-26

"For everyone has sinned; we all fall short of God's glorious standard. Yet God, in his grace, freely makes us right in his sight. He did this through Christ Jesus when he freed us from the penalty for our sins."

"For God presented Jesus as the sacrifice for sin. People are made right with God when they believe that Jesus sacrificed his life, shedding his blood."

"This sacrifice shows that God was being fair when he held back and did not punish those who sinned in times past, for he was looking ahead and including them in what he would do in this present time."

"God did this to demonstrate his righteousness, for he himself is fair and just, and <u>he makes sinners right in his sight when they believe in Jesus</u>."

Romans 4:13-15

"Clearly, God's promise to give the whole earth to Abraham and his descendants was based not on his obedience to God's law, but on a right relationship with God that comes by faith."

"If God's promise is only for those who obey the law, then faith is not necessary and the promise is pointless."

"For the law always brings punishment on those who try to obey it. (The only way to avoid breaking the law is to have no law to break!)"

Romans 5:1, 2

"Therefore, since we have been made right in God's sight by faith, we have peace with God because of what Jesus Christ our Lord has done for us."

"Because of our faith, Christ has brought us into this place of undeserved privilege where we now stand, and we confidently and joyfully look forward to sharing God's glory."

Romans 5:20-21
"God's law was given so that all people could see how sinful they were. But as people sinned more and more, God's wonderful grace became more abundant."

"So just as sin ruled over all people and brought them to death, now God's wonderful grace rules instead, giving us right standing with God and resulting in eternal life through Jesus Christ our Lord."

Romans 10:9, 10
"If you openly declare that Jesus is Lord and believe in your heart that God raised him from the dead, you will be saved."

"For it is by believing in your heart that you are made right with God, and it is by openly declaring your faith that you are saved."

Romans 10:13
"For 'Everyone who calls on the name of the Lord will be saved.'"

So Who do You call Upon to Secure your Future?

If it's not THE BANKER (**Christ**), we have a problem, Houston. There is no other banker available to secure your soul both now and in the future except The Banker — Jesus Christ. All other options cannot guarantee you any security and a retirement package of such magnitude and grandeur. Don't be fooled by the false news you hear from other establishments in the business of soul-winning. They just cannot deliver.

The only way to the Father is through the Son (John 14:6). This statement from the Bible holds true no matter what. It's better because FDIC, according to God's Word, stands for Father Destined In Christ. How's that for a different synonym application?

I often read about other religions, and I am amused how they take a few words from the Bible and conjure up a story that starts in the right direction, then quickly takes a rabbit trail and miss the whole point of the message. They inject fables that fall short of the actual biblical explanation and consistently fail to provide the entire Truth. I know you're not supposed to talk about politics or religion, but our salvation is a very serious subject that needs our undivided, immediate attention.

Waiting to talk about our faith just before we die is not recommended. Thinking you still have time to decide to accept Christ could easily be missed should it be put off, and then you die suddenly. The decision to accept Christ is only available while we are living. Remember that!

So When is the Right Time for Salvation?

2 Corinthians 6:1-2
"As God's partners, we beg you not to accept this marvelous gift of God's kindness and then ignore it. For God says, At just the right time, I heard you."

"On the day of salvation, I helped you."

"Indeed, the 'right time' is now. <u>Today is the day of salvation</u>."

If you're waiting until the last minute to decide — that is leaving your eternal destiny to chance. And, you might not get 'another chance' to decide for yourself. Am I trying to frighten you? I think I am. The decision to accept Christ and keep your soul positioned where you want it after death is a serious matter. Choose yourself (accept Jesus) or take your chances to experience eternal damnation personally. You certainly do have the free will to choose — but that is only while you are alive!

To have a full life and fulfill God's purpose for you requires a decision to accept Him and receive your salvation. Your acceptance begins the process to act out His Word and begin to receive the promises that are available to you because of your decision. This act of acceptance opens up a spiritual connection between you and the Lord.

When you begin this new life in Christ, doors of opportunity will start to open. Your growth will depend on how much you allow His Word to renew your thinking and fill your spirit. When you begin putting His principles into practice, the beginning of His wisdom starts to pour in and materialize. It becomes very personal as you experience God for yourself. As you progress and grow and apply His principles, your future with Him will develop and deepen, and your journey through life will begin to change for the better.

In my last book, _Stages of Life_, I explain what the Lord gave me to write about, which all came in a diagram that shows, from a biblical viewpoint, the seven stages that are available to all humanity. I marveled at the diagram God gave me because once I scribbled it on paper, only then could I understand what the Lord had prompted me to write. The visual was much easier to understand because I could refer back to it and see more clearly.

It was apparent He prompted me because the whole concept would never have entered my mind otherwise. Writing a book based on a God-given diagram was like receiving an outline in the form of a picture with the details providing what I needed to follow and then writing about my impression. I'm just not that creative on my own.

God's promises are accurate, and there are many throughout the Bible. You will soon find that you have a part to play in bringing them into reality. They don't just immediately materialize, and 'boom' they fall in front of you. God has a purpose and a plan for your life as you follow His advice. Many opportunities will reveal themselves of what your part will include. His Word, prayer and the Holy Spirit will agree and help you with the details.

The details are always in agreement with His Word, and usually, a prompting from the Holy Spirit accompanies, and you will learn to hear His voice as you continue to listen, learn, and grow in the Lord.

Today, our society likes everything instantly without wasting time to arrive at the answer they want to hear. And should the answer not be acceptable; usually disobedience follows rather than waiting and responding in obedience.

Our impatient natural attitude does not like to wait any length of time to arrive at a godly solution. The impatient person usually plows ahead without God's confirmation then blames the failed results on Him. This kind of response is NOT waiting on the Lord. As I've quoted before — 'sometimes the timing is as critical as the message,' (from a sermon by Dr. Charles Swindoll).

Don't believe for a minute God is going to answer your every whim or desire and do it immediately. He will start immediately to answer, but the best results for you may take some time to both arrange in your favor or grow you up so you can handle what He brings. The answer may need time for you to mature to correctly respond and be the help He needs.

As I discussed earlier, sometimes the answer is no, and that is not what we want to hear — silence. When we get no response, the answer is either no, or it might take a while to gather all required to make your request a reality with the best results possible. It could be that your growth is slow in becoming more Christlike and requires several more opportunities and ample time for you to become more mature.

The Lord almost always provides more than we need, and He brings a greater blessing than we prayed for in the beginning. His answer to prayer may be quite involved or next to impossible without your participation and cooperation. Also, if you're sitting around waiting for an answer, it could be your participation is required to complete your part in helping make your prayer a reality.

In addition, we should be careful what we pray because events may take place that makes the journey more complicated — especially if I'm not ready to handle the blessing. Remember, the Lord wants to bless us and answer our prayer requests, but He prefers to give us a blessed future that will project us in His direction and according to His timing. Receiving a blessing that you're not ready to handle can be quite harmful.

Our prayers should align with Scripture, so we don't ask for something contrary to His will. In addition to this idea, we should also consider that since He is in charge, we should trust Him by faith and wait until His answer comes. Always consider that our rushing towards an answer might place us in front of God's intent and mess up His perfect timing.

There is a Story in the Bible regarding King Hezekiah

The following verses from 2 Kings explain the need for our trust in the Lord in greater detail:

2 Kings 16:20
"When Ahaz died (the father of Hezekiah), he was buried with his ancestors in the City of David. Then his son Hezekiah became the next king."

2 Kings 18:5
"Hezekiah trusted in the Lord, the God of Israel. There was no one like him among all the kings of Judah, either before or after his time."

Much Later in the Life of King Hezekiah

2 Kings 20:1-2
"About that time Hezekiah became deathly ill, and the prophet Isaiah son of Amoz went to visit him."

"He gave the king this message: 'This is what the Lord says: Set your affairs in order, for you are going to die. You will not recover from this illness.'"

"When Hezekiah heard this, he turned his face to the wall and prayed to the Lord,"

If we could have heard King Hezekiah pray, I'll bet it was a prayer of panic and desperation that unfolded. Who would want to know when they were going to die, especially when everything was going so well? I would certainly turn my face to the wall and pray — probably with crocodile (large) tears. It would probably have been a one-word prayer too — Help!

Because of King Hezekiah's Prayer the Lord Granted him Additional Time on Earth

2 Kings 20:5
"Go back to Hezekiah, the leader of my people. Tell him, 'This is what the Lord, the God of your ancestor David, says: I have heard your prayer and seen your tears. I will heal you, and three days from now you will get out of bed and go to the Temple of the Lord.'"

"Go back to Hezekiah and tell him, 'This is what the Lord, the God of your ancestor David, says: I have heard your prayer and seen your tears. I will add fifteen years to your life'"

And the Story continues —

2 Chronicles 32:33
"When Hezekiah died, he was buried in the upper area of the royal cemetery, and all Judah and Jerusalem honored him at his death. And his son Manasseh became the next king."

Jeremiah 15:4
"Because of the wicked things Manasseh son of Hezekiah, king of Judah, did in Jerusalem, I will make my people an object of horror to all the kingdoms of the earth."

This story of King Hezekiah relates to a prayer he made requesting additional years to live. It was granted, but the results were devastating. King Hezekiah was a great king and served the Lord well. His son Manasseh (a direct result of the additional years) was the worst king in Judah ever recorded in biblical history.

The fifteen years of added life for Hezekiah produced a son that became an evil king. Had Hezekiah gone along with the Lord's original plan, then the corruption and evil brought to God's people would never have been brought to Jerusalem. So, what is the moral of this story and the events that followed? I believe it is a message for us all. Stick to God's best, and don't insist on your alternative.

Had King Hezekiah remained content with the timeframe God had designated for his life, the son Manasseh and all the wrongdoings he introduced would never have taken place. Our wanting something different from what God has planned can lead to more problems than we can imagine. Maybe God's timing is the very best, even if we perceive things differently.

This example from Scripture gives us a clear picture that God knows best and should be careful of what we ask for in prayer. I believe we should always stipulate that we want what is in God's best interest and ours in the final outcome. Trusting the Lord to provide the very best, and learning to trust He knows better than we do!

Trusting God in all situations and circumstances requires faith that He will do precisely what He promises in the Bible. Our understanding isn't usually very complete and, of course, we would certainly like to know beforehand, but that usually isn't the case. Just know in your heart that God always wants the very best for you, and He will always be faithful to delivery the very best in His desired results.

God doesn't provide a road map to show us how our life will take place — even though we would like to know ahead of time. He doesn't tell us beforehand what the outcome will look like, but to put our trust in Him. He does provide wisdom and help when we face a problem and is more than willing to guide us through it. As we learn to follow His leading, which can be a little frightening sometimes, His leadership is never failing and always provides the best results as we respond in obedience.

Taking the route, He suggests, won't unveil everything that lies ahead. This is a walk of faith, meaning we first take each step all the way to the end of the road. But, we can rest assured it will be the path He wants us to take. It requires faith in Him and lots of practice to grow our trust in Him.

Trusting God requires our growing in faith, and faith-building is a process and not a one-time event that is quickly over during our time of travels through life. It takes place continually and is confirmed one degree of faith built upon another, so we become more mature during our walk.

Learning more about the Lord draws us closer because we continue to learn His heart and better understand how His wisdom so brilliantly is woven all through our creation. Through the power of the Holy Spirit, His presence enables humankind to more easily travel through life and provides the opportunity to receive the blessings God intends for us to experience before spending Eternity with Him.

Chapter 8

Does the Bible Really
Have the Answer?

Now, let me share a nugget of gold that has taken me into a place I did not know existed for most of my life. This new Bible understanding began as I started to write books. I found that a not-so-talented writer can glean a great deal of knowledge if one can learn to listen to the Lord. Being relatively slow to listen, I am learning to remain quiet more and seek the voice of the Lord better now than ever before.

I had some knowledge of learning how to listen to the voice of the Lord but did not understand what all that meant. It is challenging for a person when their mind is traveling at warp speed to take the time to listen. People like me would rather talk than listen because they are mentally traveling through life at such a speed they don't pause long enough to hear anything very well.

My son has this same problem, and once I ask him what it felt like to have your mind loudly traveling at high volume all the time. His explanation gave me insight that reflected directly on my situation. He told me his mind was like a computer running all the time and no way to shut it off. Even sleep was difficult for him because of this problem.

He will practice relaxing his body when he lays down to sleep. His statement caused me to think.

As I thought about myself, I realized he was correct in my situation as well. I didn't know how to shut my computer off, and I realized I didn't even know how to slow it down. Once I started praying about it, I found the Lord could help me respond in the right direction. I started praying differently and began practicing how to listen to the still quiet voice of God on purpose. I still practice today to slow down and allow the Holy Spirit to whisper into my spirit. I am growing closer to the Lord as a direct result.

Now there are times when I realize the Lord is talking directly to me and flooding my spirit with His promptings. My deeper relationship with Him has dramatically influenced my life and allowed me to communicate my thoughts into words with better understanding and clarity. This realization became apparent with my first book, _Coming Before the LORD_, which caused me to listen more intently than I ever had before.

That's when the Lord began, or I began to listen, prompting me to write down what was inside of me, causing me frustration with my lack of ability to express on paper what was inside. I had not realized until then the Lord was giving me promptings that included information, book cover designs, and picture outlines that instructed me how to layout an entire book. The realization this was taking place amazed me.

Not being a talented writer soon moved out of my thinking to be replaced with the idea that anything is possible with God if you will but let Him instruct you. I learned that the Bible does have the answer and that I needed to further indulge in His Word and learn more about what was in this fantastic book. My actions followed, and the depth of wisdom obtained has been so revealing.

I have applied numerous scriptural principles for many years and benefited greatly from them over my lifetime. But now, I was learning to go deeper into the wisdom of God and see for myself the nuggets of gold that were scattered throughout the entire book. As I grew and listened to His promptings, I began to write them down and save them in a box for future reference. Little did I know these written messages would compile my first book.

These nuggets of gold are available to each believer. What awaits depends on how hard you are willing to look for them. Unlike gold nuggets from the earth, these treasures of wisdom have a tremendous effect on our future. Gathering them and learning first-hand will provide each believer with the true knowledge and understanding they need. These nuggets give insight into situations that unveil available solutions that can be applied in today's world.

I never realized before there was so much wisdom available from a book written so long ago. I believe we think being old is outdated, and when viewed on the surface, it is easy to believe just that. The exciting part is that we don't have to read it in old English anymore. With all the new translations, the beauty of indulging in the Word of God better reveals tremendous principles that work every time they are used. That old book has many shared stories, some in parables, but all to help the people of that time better understand.

Once you better understand the applications and intentions, the principles still apply to living life today. The location is different, but the principles are the same. Applying God's Word reveals much power in application because the results end in changes only God can perform. And with the new translations, our understanding is much better met and allows us to see more realistically than ever before.

It is a miracle because the principles of God are powerful, and we can experience them today just like they did many years ago. His principles do not become void over time, nor do they fail in application. Our answer to every question can be found in the Bible. It will require us to learn how to dig for gold nuggets of wisdom that each believer can find. You can experience the benefits of these nuggets by applying God's principles, and you will significantly benefit from its value with the application.

Those many nuggets you find are scattered throughout the entire Bible. What a gold mine the Bible turns out to be, and once you get your spiritual awakening (accepting the Lord), you will be provided a helper, the Holy Spirit, to assist you in gathering the wisdom you need for the betterment of your life. It's all free and available to every believer without hesitation (James 1:5; 3:17).

Your mining skills become better each time you enter the Bible and dig for gold. As you accumulate wisdom and apply each principle, your future will become more on track as you move forward through life. By the time you grow in the Lord, you will have matured in age as well. Your accumulation of gold is quite valuable and needs to be shared with others. This fortune you've accumulated is meant to be given away because there is an endless supply available to all.

The foundational truths found in God's Word will always come true and withstand the test of time. Every word spoken will come to pass when used because His Word is alive and will result in what it was intended for by God (the word is sharper than a two-edged sword) (Hebrews 4:12). God's intent for His Word can change anything according to His will — no matter what. Never think that something written from the Lord is only ink on paper. It is unfailing and very profitable to each believer.

His timeless gems are nuggets of gold that bring blessings to the believer from the Provider directly as we are obedient to His Word. Our instruction book has vivid illustrations written in words of wisdom provided for our pleasure, assistance, and usage.

Knowing the result will become a means of understanding that will catapult us into His will for our lives. Each nugget of wisdom has purpose and reason beyond our abilities to process in our natural thinking (flesh). His ways far exceed the capabilities we could muster up and will escalate us to a level of amazement we could only imagine.

The plans of the Lord take us on the pathway that brings completion and blessings we're not capable of reaching on our own. Our God enables us to travel through life with His assistance and His abilities unobtainable without Him. God's wisdom far exceeds our thinking and unfolds before us as we travel by faith into the unknown (Isaiah 55:9). Our guide, the Holy Spirit, will take us on the road less traveled, but that is only because many others will only dare to follow.

Think about the Following Scripture

Colossians 2:8

"Don't let anyone capture you with empty philosophies and high-sounding nonsense that come from human thinking and from the spiritual powers of this world, rather than from Christ."

To give you an example of what God can do, I want to take you on a trip through Scripture that will provide you with several snapshot photos of what I'm talking about. This trip began early in my life when I attended Vacation Bible School one summer. Each day focused on praising God, and the teachers gave many stories taken from the Bible.

My spiritual beginning was when I accepted Jesus as my Lord and Savior during this summer (1951). This one-act opened my spiritual eyes even as a young boy of six. I can remember becoming aware of the adults in this church and could sense their honesty and intent. I could determine and sense some things were wrong, but I didn't understand or know why. As I watched them each day, I would visually see their lifestyle, which revealed a great deal about them and taught me to become aware of discernment and what I was seeing from a spiritual viewpoint.

I thought it strange they would talk one way at church but were different during the week. My parents allowed me to go with them to get fuel for the car, maybe get something welded on a trailer, or it could be to pick up an equipment part at the dealership in town. There were trips to purchase feed for our animals or a day to work on equipment in the barn, go to the grocery store in town each week was fun, and pick up meat from our food locker, and visiting with folks all along the way.

If my grandma went along, she always purchased a dozen donuts and gave my sister and I one each. They were sometimes warm and trying to eat just one was very difficult for me. I really liked donuts, ice cream, grandma's banana cake, fried chicken, mashed potatoes smothered with chicken gravy, corn on the cob, ect. Really, the only thing I didn't like was to go hungry. You get the picture, right?

My parents would purchase needed items to work on the farm, completing the many tasks that needed attention. Some of the tasks were doctoring the cattle for pink eye, feeding the livestock, making sure the cattle trough had sufficient water, farming the land, planting seed for future needed crops, repairing the barbed wire fence, or maybe putting up an electric fence to contain the cattle being pastured on the property. Daily gather eggs from the hen house, burn the trash, or clean the clothesline so mom could hang out the clothes to dry she had just washed. Each of these tasks were exciting to me and kept me happy and enjoying living on a farm.

Nevertheless, the folks we came into contact with along the way always seemed to have a spirit about them, and it would materialize in short order. It didn't take long for me to figure out much about them by just being in their presence. I didn't realize I was discerning anything, but I found out my sense of discernment was right as time went on. I learned that this gift would provide an excellent way to avoid trouble and trust God to give me better insight into people I was around.

As I grew up, I continued to attend church, and when we moved to the city, I was turning twelve. This change was difficult because I left everything I loved about the farm into a new environment that I didn't enjoy much. It relocated me into a strange place where people were very different, and many were questionable in their faith and beliefs.

Church in the city became my point of contact with the Lord, but I was still young and vulnerable to new and deceitful ways I had never encountered before. My sense of discernment was a precious tool in sizing up people and their intentions. I didn't follow God's narrow path very well because I was not aware there was any more to following after God than going to church and trying to always do the right thing.

My 'religion' was helpful, but it did not fulfill my personal spiritual needs. I kept trying to be good, with limited success but never accomplished much beyond my own thinking. I didn't know any better. I talked to the Lord most of the time and often felt like I would have been in serious trouble if He weren't there with me. My grandparents were now 125 miles away, and I didn't have their input to help me deal with life anymore.

As I became older, I learned more about the Bible but had never heard about something more than attending church and following a set of rules from what the Bible said. I assumed that the rest was up to me, and allowing the Holy Spirit to help me was never discussed in any detail. At least not that I remember. I understood that I was to be good and act a certain way, but I didn't know what that meant or exactly how it all worked.

After I got married, the pressure increased, and once we went for marriage counseling, I began to hear new things about the Lord and what He had made available to all believers. The church I was attending believed the Bible was full of great truths, and there were times a miracle would take place during service. This church was loaded with people like me who were hungry for more of the Lord but didn't know where to look.

As I started to apply many principles from the Bible, I discovered where my help was and began my application process. On many occasions, I would read the Word of God, then believe it would come to pass, and then become amazed that it worked.

Money was difficult for me to release to the Lord and incorporate Scripture into my life. I tried to follow after Scripture as I thought best. I began to learn more as I grew in the knowledge of the Lord. I would practice a verse, and events would start happening that became manifest in my life. This experience gave me assurance that God was real and His Word was true!

The whole time I was sure I knew the Lord because we talked all the time. I didn't realize that I needed to follow after His Word and make it a part of my lifestyle in real-time. Otherwise, nothing would take place, and no real, lasting change came. As I continued learning more and applying more principles, I could see that God was more real than I ever imagined. He really was alive and well and waiting for me to open the door to His presence in every area of my life — not just some.

Then I heard about relationships and discovered I was trying to be religious. I learned first-hand that religion doesn't work very well. I learned that relationship was what I was looking for the whole time. Talk about life-changing! This wisdom began a much more profound respect for God and released in me the Holy Spirit empowering me, bringing an entirely new understanding and confidence.

The renewing of my mind began to saturate my spirit as I plunged into God's Word. My relationship became so real, and I was so appreciative. Finally, I didn't feel alone anymore, and my understanding enlarged to a scope I was not aware existed. The Lord began changing me, and the more I grew and allowed Him to work in my life, the more excited I became.

My obedience grew as I learned and followed His guidance. My life was changing for the better all the time. There was real hope for me now, and I loved almost every minute of it. Yes, there were some moments where He called me to mend fences, and I would compare them to the barbed wire we strung on our farm to contain the cattle. Somewhat prickly with great potential to damage my flesh if I wasn't careful.

Of course, the lessons I learned were not all enjoyable, but they certainly helped me grow and trust in the Lord to a greater level (Hebrews 12:11). Many benefits came from my obedience to the promptings of the Holy Spirit. I hadn't realized how disobedient I had been until I sold out to the Lord in every area of my life. Those tiny rooms we hide in our hearts don't go away without His help. And, His help requires us to give them over to Him in prayer and allow Him to make the needed adjustments.

I found out first-hand the Lord will do a work in us if we follow after Him. I found that I was waiting for the answer to fall into my life. I learned that my answer was in the Bible, and I was standing still by not seeking a solution. I learned my seeking His help required me to search the Scriptures and pray. And in doing so, I could find what I needed to get me through another set of circumstances that were obstructing my path.

James 1:2-8
"Dear brothers and sisters, when troubles of any kind come your way, consider it an opportunity for great joy. For you know that when your faith is tested, your endurance has a chance to grow."

"So let it grow, for when your endurance is fully developed, you will be perfect and complete, needing nothing."

"If you need wisdom, ask our generous God, and he will give it to you. He will not rebuke you for asking. But when you ask him, be sure that your faith is in God alone. Do not waver, for a person with divided loyalty is as unsettled as a wave of the sea that is blown and tossed by the wind."

"Such people should not expect to receive anything from the Lord. Their loyalty is divided between God and the world, and they are unstable in everything they do."

It's kind of like sitting at home while being unemployed, hoping a job will come in the front door when it should be us out looking for a job and seeking employment. God doesn't serve us — we serve Him. Taking that into consideration provides us with a path to follow that leads to success and many blessings. We don't need to develop an attitude of entitlement, as many do, but rather an attitude of servanthood (Romans 12:1).

We are to serve our God by moving in His direction and remembering the price Jesus suffered in His obedience to the Father. I find it strange that Jesus benefited from suffering as He acted in obedience to the Father. And, it is revealed in Scripture that our suffering to be obedient to God is nothing out of the ordinary (Hebrews 5:8 & 9).

Growing in the Lord does cause our flesh to squirm, but the saying, 'more of Jesus and less of me' is a good view of what is needed. Our flesh would rather do what makes it feel good, but the downside, and there are many, the flesh will never be satisfied. While denying the flesh to be obedient to Scripture will cause some discomfort initially, the rewards found at completion will be far greater than any discomfort you will experience (Romans 8:1).

I read some time back that our fear of the future was a tool that Satan loves to use to cause us to hold back and not step out in faith. The article indicated that 98% of what we fear would never take place. So, if that is true, surely we can trust the Lord during that 98% and reduce the level of doubt to 2%. I don't have any evidence to prove this, but it has had great validity so far in my own life.

Fearing the unknown causes us to exhibit no faith, and since faith is what pleases God, we find ourselves hopeless and unchallenged by life's circumstances. Did you ever think that circumstances are allowed by God to cause us to turn to Him for help? Maybe your present circumstances are there to cause you to move in another direction. Just possibly, God is prompting you to step out in faith and follow after His leading rather than suffer through on your own.

Could it be possible you're remaining where you are is not in your best interest? The Lord is constantly moving in our lives to motivate us. Our choosing a direction toward Him will provide His help in action and cause you to grow in understanding and faith. This moving of God is a good thing and shows us His concern for our wellbeing. God loves us, and He is eager to draw us closer to Himself.

My life experiences have given me many opportunities to find out. It has proven out to me that the Bible God provided us has the answer to our every need. What I used to call problems are now viewed as His promptings to move me off dead center and reach out in faith rather than suffer through the consequences I encounter by myself. His ways certainly are not my ways, and His solutions usually don't seem reasonable to me initially.

Just like you, my life has been full of unwanted circumstances that can't be ignored, dealt with by yourself, or they can be approached with Scripture. The scriptural approach hasn't always been seen as reasonable from my viewpoint, but acting out in obedience to His Word has never failed me. That experience has been very encouraging and brings me much comfort in tackling life and planning for the future.

I even find myself going to Scripture more as I mature in the knowledge of His Word because I know my answer must be in there somewhere. And, when I find the solution, I am confident the application of His principle will yield me the best possible results. Our life is filled with many opportunity to experience God working in our lives. It trains us in the truth of Scripture and develops in us the wisdom and character God has provided to see us through successfully.

Our life is filled with newness from the Lord daily and a great chance to grow and expand our limited knowledge of our surroundings and the people we encounter each day. I don't believe there is a dull moment in serving the Lord. I see only an opportunity to expand beyond ourselves into the likeness of Christ. A welcomed change that far exceeds our expectations with experiences that are much better than traveling life alone.

Life will challenge everyone that's traveling through. Many challenges are different, but the majority are similar in our everyday living. Searching for the future brings excitement and allows for insecurity because our past experiences may not bring any knowledge of which way to go. We all, of course, apply ourselves to meet the challenges, and sometimes we learn as we go rather than reflect on our past to give us direction.

Our free will gives us the choice to choose our future. There is great freedom in making your mind up about the future you desire. Knowing what Scripture declares about obedience provides a picture of what to expect based on our decision-making. It also gives a good picture of our future should we neglect God's help. This overview is all good and brings excellent opportunities that continually come to your attention to choose how you want to go.

When I listen to people, I hear them saying they are quite capable of moving forward without help from anyone. They tell me they have been listening to others their whole life and want to start making their own decisions from this point on. Relying on someone else is exactly what they want to get away from — not go back to. Besides, they are strong and determined enough alone and don't need to rely on someone else. Relying on a religious crutch tells others how weak you are and I'm not weak or helpless.

If Christianity is perceived as a crutch, then I can see their viewpoint. But, Christianity is not a crutch, but rather helpful for you to initiate the principles so you have the promises God provides that can bring great success. If someone were to give you a map that would give you an assurance of victory in what lies ahead, would that be an expression of weakness or a sign of foresight?

I believe it would exhibit to others your wisdom, and the results would be an excellent example for others to follow. By definition, meekness is power under control. A stallion that is ridden with a saddle and bridle is undoubtedly not weakened by the added equipment. Instead, he is trained to have guidance so the rider can better select the direction ahead that provides the best results for both.

It isn't much different for us as humans. Our reliance on God only empowers us to move forward in the right direction and reap the benefits from applying biblical principles and obtaining the best overall results. God doesn't take over our lives He equips us by helping us make the most of our circumstances and reap the rewards at the conclusion. God is our helper — not our dictator.

To view life from our human viewpoint only severely limits our vision and allows for our partial blindness to obstruct the pathway. The Lord created us, and He knows how we operate and even how we think. He is aware that traveling alone is not recommended and, in His mercy and grace, has provided us an option that was not available until the Holy Spirit of God was released in each believer.

Weakness could be defined as exhibiting very little power to storm through life with minimal good results to show at the end. This endeavor includes our determination, willpower, and application of strength to move forward in our chosen direction. What if there are obstacles unknown to us? What will one do when something stronger than you blocks your path? How can you overpower something operating in the spiritual realm, and your physical strength, no matter how strong, cannot deflect or defeat it?

These are real obstacles, and we each face these every day and in our future. They are present and functional, and we must be aware of their presence and how to combat them. Without the Lord in our life, we are powerless and without weapons to fight against them. You can't fight against something stronger than you and win, but with God's help and His weapons of engagement, we can overcome.

The Bible stipulates in Ephesians chapter 6, who our enemy is in the spiritual realm and what it takes to overpower its onslaught. Every person living on earth has these same obstacles, but believers have the ability, by choice, to engage in battle and be victorious. Without these spiritual weapons, we are powerless no matter what one may think. Physical strength cannot overcome spiritual enemies!

Check Out Scripture to What I'm Saying

Ephesians 6:1-18
"A final word: Be strong in the Lord and in his mighty power. Put on all of God's armor so that you will be able to stand firm against all strategies of the devil."

"For we are not fighting against flesh-and-blood enemies, but against evil rulers and authorities of the unseen world, against mighty powers in this dark world, and against evil spirits in the heavenly places."

"Therefore, put on every piece of God's armor so you will be able to resist the enemy in the time of evil. Then after the battle you will still be standing firm. Stand your ground, putting on the belt of truth and the body armor of God's righteousness."

"For shoes, put on the peace that comes from the Good News so that you will be fully prepared. In addition to all of these, hold up the shield of faith to stop the fiery arrows of the devil."

"Put on salvation as your helmet, and take the sword of the Spirit, which is the word of God. Pray in the Spirit at all times and on every occasion. Stay alert and be persistent in your prayers for all believers everywhere."

Romans 8:26
"And the Holy Spirit helps us in our weakness. For example, we don't know what God wants us to pray for. But the Holy Spirit prays for us with groanings that cannot be expressed in words."

1 Corinthians 6:25
"This foolish plan of God is wiser than the wisest of human plans, and God's weakness is stronger than the greatest of human strength."

Without the Bible to guide us, wisdom with great instructions, and principles to live our lives, we are but mere targets roaming around unaware of who's shooting at us but feeling the evidence of their evil presence. The Bible gives us a powerful approach to life and a history of proven results. It reveals our history with Bible characters, real people, and examples of triumphs and failures.

2 Corinthians 12:9
"Each time he said, 'My grace is all you need. My power works best in weakness.' So now I am glad to boast about my weaknesses, so that the power of Christ can work through me."

Paul revealed in the above Scripture that our weaknesses in our human nature (Romans 6:19) are limitations, yet in this great void, Christ can strengthen and work through us. Our weaknesses are present in our flesh just because of our natural makeup. This void is there for a reason because it provides a tremendous opportunity to invite Christ in and eliminate that weakness and utilize His strength!

In Psalm 136:23, we read that God remembered us in our weakness and gave us provisions to overcome with His help. God's love (agape) for humankind is quite evident throughout the Bible and gives us samples of His care and preparation to help every believer during their lifetime. He didn't forget — He planned ahead for us.

We read in Hebrews chapter 11 about examples of faith exhibited by those that preceded us. Their great victories were obtained as God enabled them to move under His power to accomplish the given task. They did not operate alone, and it was not their human strength alone that gave them victory. Each moved forward in faith, still not capable of victory based on their own power, but realizing their weaknesses, then calling up the Lord and moving ahead anyway.

We can conclude that we are much weaker without the Lord working in our lives. His instruction book, the Bible, provides us with the needed wisdom to show us the way to meet life's challenges head-on and that He allows for the necessary help to be successful and prosperous during our visit here. His empowerment provides us the strength we need to be overcomers.

So if faith is viewed to be a crutch, then we should seek the Truth of God's Word and see the accurate picture. Poor visibility can be avoided in Christ, and a bright future can be yours. Move toward the Lord in your travels and be determined you will find out for yourself.

Taking God at His Word will exercise your faith and increase your trust in what He can do through you. There is ample evidence in the application of biblical principles by the results. Those telling you otherwise choose to remain in darkness rather than seek after the true Light, which can only be found in the Bible.

Chapter 9

How Did I Become Involved in All of This?

I very much like the above question because I know the answer. What is the answer, you ask? It is not difficult, nor is it a mystery. Scripture reveals to humankind the origin of man as we read in Genesis. All of creation has been designed and created by God. We can see the evidence of Him all around (Romans 1:20)!

God involved you in all of creation. This life on earth with other humans in various languages, skin colors, different locations, various climates, numerous lifestyles, cultures, shapes and sizes, and even appearance. We each get to experience an extensive sampling of life as we travel through. There are no exceptions! This assortment of people provides us with endless challenges and many opportunities to expand our understanding, tolerance, abilities, learning, and spiritual growth, including many failures and successes, difficult circumstances, opportunities, opinions based on our self-evaluation, acceptance, rejections, patience, etc.

You get the picture. Way more than you bargained for, I'm sure. Yes, you were placed into a family with parents that were not of your choosing. There was never an opportunity for you to select or approve and make the selection yourself. Maybe you also have a brother or sister that came into the group, and you can't figure out if they actually came from the same gene stockpile as you.

As you well know by now, you can't do a whole lot about much of anything to select your beginning life on earth. The best approach is to start from where you are and decide where you want to go. Some avenues are easier than others, but you can be certain difficulties will appear in your future travels. The road ahead is cluttered with obstacles that need your attention. Trying to overcome them will result in a past cluttered with successes and failures. And as a result, you are signed up for life on earth in the here and now.

Resolving past issues will give you more freedom to leave the unwanted hurt you encountered behind. The learning you'll receive builds character in you to provide you with experience that will assist in handling the future. Efforts to incorporate God's principles will clarify direction and give you good advice. Then, you must exert yourself and trudge forward, meeting your future head-on.

Your approval was not needed to cast you into life, but you have a choice from here on. And remember, your selections are critical in deciding your future and the path you choose to take. The Bible identifies the physical world we inhabit and can physically see and the spiritual world we cannot see. Scripture tells us the facts about our environment and what to expect. It also provides godly principles to follow that guide your choices to get the best possible results.

It seems that we each are given numerous situations that require us to select the direction that's best for us. And yes, some difficulties challenge us and must be dealt with to get through and gain a favorable outcome. This scenario is just the way things are — realism at its best.

We each find many similarities, but we also experience many differences. The nature of our circumstances requires actions on our part to proceed forward, which determine the path we are going to take. The more you know ahead of time, the better selection you will make. That's why it is so critical we learn and apply Scripture to our decision-making. The Bible provides superior wisdom in dealing with life that will ease the journey and make it more enjoyable.

You have been signed up for this life to fulfill God's purpose on earth. That means He has a plan and a specific purpose for you. Working alongside each of us He will provide the opportunity to release the Spirit of God within us (1 Corinthians 2:10-12). Our abilities and wisdom in Christ far exceed our capabilities alone and are only a request away. Our acceptance of the Lord in our lives opens up a dimension to living that is unknown without Him.

Your involvement in all this was intentional because God has a plan. His plan is massive because He is dealing with the whole world and each person in it. Your part may seem very small, but it directly influences the entire plan of God. Ignoring Him will produce poor results in fulfilling your purpose on earth. Why? Because God has chosen people to carry out His working on the earth. He could do the work Himself, but He chooses to call upon us.

Besides, without God's principles applied, we will walk in darkness, never seeing the whole picture and what we need to be doing to benefit from His Son's death, burial, and resurrection. His dying on the cross opened up opportunities for each believer, not possible before Christ. The Lord has provided all we need to live a fulfilled life here, then a glorious future and with Him in Eternity once it all ends (1 Corinthians 2:9).

What part could you possibly have in a plan so massive? We need to remember that every word from the Bible will come to pass (Isaiah 46:10). Not one single word will be overlooked or unfulfilled that you read in the Bible. And, God desires that you will follow His leading, apply His biblical principles to your life, and grow in your understanding of Him and His purpose.

Believers that practice their faith are changed continually to become more like Christ in their actions, nature, and character. When a believer lives around people who haven't chosen to follow the Lord, you are probably the only Christ they currently are seeing. That means your purpose is quite evident and extremely critical and beneficial as the Lord fulfills His love for humanity in bringing them back to Himself through your example.

The job you now have is probably an excellent opportunity for you to witness to the unbeliever in a tangible way that is meaningful to them. I don't mean with religious talk that is offensive to them, but a Christlike character that portrays the gifts and characteristics that set you apart with good examples of a believer.

This example of a Christian doesn't mean you need to pack around a ten-pound Schofield Bible, a bumper sticker on your car, or body dressings that cause you to appear like a preacher on the move that might use physical force to get his point across. I have not yet found an unbeliever that is open to being force-fed something they aren't interested in anyway.

We all have difficult situations, and your witness to those around you needs to let others see the benefits of the Gospel of Christ working in your life and making a noticeable difference. This is especially true should you go through a crisis with the character of Christ, your example will speak volumes because of your positive attitude and faith in the One who will see you through without fail. These are the signs of a believer that others see very clearly.

So what's your purpose? Your purpose is to exhibit Christ working in you that cause your actions, attitude, personality, and gifts at a visible level that all can see. Your life is critical to most unbelievers because this showing of Scripture in action speaks to them right where their soul is located. Your example reaches deep into their being where the Holy Spirit of God wants to live and make a difference in their lives as well.

That means you might be the witness God uses to plant a seed, maybe water it and be responsible for plowing a way for God to cause them to reap from your spiritual farming skills. You never fully know how the Lord may work and use you during your lifetime. There are so many ways He utilizes opportunities to speak to the unbelieving. He wants their soul to be saved and goes to extraordinary measures to make it possible for all of humanity.

Then what might be in your future as a believer? My mother-in-law used a phrase that has always caused me to smile. That phrase is: 'You just never know.' That is correct. We have no idea what lies ahead and how the Lord might use us. For sure, He will use you mightily if you are available and obedient to His Word!

There have been a few other things my mother-in-law has told me, but I will save them for another story. They, too, have caused me to see life from a slightly different viewpoint. It amazes me that each person God saves has wisdom beyond themselves and, at times, doesn't realize how much they have changed in their character and way of thinking.

I have been blessed in my lifetime to meet many people that usher in God's ideas and obediently respond to life situations God has allowed in their travels. I'm convinced the Lord has a great sense of humor because of the many resolutions God has provided to others as they listen for that still small voice He chooses to use in talking to us. Some of the humor has kept me laughing my entire life. And, there is more to come!

God speaks in many different ways that include His Word, dreams, other people, a new thought or idea that comes to mind, situations, mystery and prominent happenings during circumstances, a sermon at church, etc. The ways are usually subtle, and we even miss Him if we're not paying attention. Simple events during the day might collectively relate to His desire for your life that can be easily overlooked. God usually does not enter the picture by sending a magnificent happening that will marvel the world.

Our God utilizes those everyday happenings to lead us into prayer and a desire for His solution to enter whatever way He is allowed by the person needing a message from Him. That's why His talking to us is referred to as a still, small voice. God surrounds His people with Himself through the Holy Spirit that is working in the earth today.

As we make ourselves available to Him, our hearing and sensing His presence give us promptings to adjust our lives to His leading. Never learning to approach Him or hear His voice leaves us moving forward with limited direction. I'm talking about a relationship with our Creator. It isn't just trying to interpret Scripture alone that gives us direction — it's our relationship with Him!

Putting on our spiritual ears is similar to receiving our spiritual eyesight. It's a God thing, and He is instrumental in causing His Spirit to come alive in our spirit. Receiving His Holy Spirit is essential in learning to communicate with the Lord. Without Him, we remain in darkness and unable to see where He is working all around us. Communication is a two-way conversation that takes more than just talking to ourselves.

A conversation with the Lord means we must listen as well. If we're the only one talking, it's a one-way conversation with no regard for the other person. Listening to the Lord is something we must cultivate and learn how to do. Our God desires to communicate back, not just listen to us all the time. I wonder how many close friends we would have if we were the only one talking all the time?

For some reason, we humans think that since we can't see Him with our natural eyes, He must be a figment of our imagination or some ghost that lives in the sky somewhere that wants to only listen to everything we have to say. Such is not the case. The Lord desires to fellowship with us and develop a close relationship that will continue to grow and flourish over time.

He is as real as every object you see with the natural eye and then some. He isn't a figment of our imagination or someone we decide in our mind based on what little we know about Him. He is a real God, the Creator of the Universe, that has come to earth in human form (Jesus) and lived among us. His Holy Spirit is His Spirit choosing to live in man and provide a personality of power that wants to operate within each believer and help us move and exist with Him as our helper.

As you read through the Bible, God's character repeatedly reveals that He desires to save everyone so they can experience a better life on earth and a splendid eternity with Him — forever! He isn't some prophet who lived long ago and has gone away, never to be seen or heard from again. He is not dead or buried in a grave somewhere. He is alive and active and is bringing into completion His plan for humanity.

John 3:16 has been used so much that I don't think we realize the sincerity of God in what is being said. The solution is extremely simple, and anyone can accept Christ on their own if they will but believe! God loves us and became a sacrifice in the form of Jesus to save us from all harm. Read this Scripture in more detail and see for yourself what God did to get us back into a relationship with Him.

John 3:13-21

"No one has ever gone to heaven and returned. But the Son of Man (Jesus) has come down from heaven. And as Moses lifted up the bronze snake on a pole in the wilderness, so the Son of Man must be lifted up, so that everyone who believes in him will have eternal life."

"For this is how God loved the world: He gave his one and only Son, so that everyone who believes in him will not perish but have eternal life. God sent his Son into the world not to judge the world, but to save the world through him."

"There is no judgment against anyone who believes in him. But anyone who does not believe in him has already been judged for not believing in God's one and only Son."

"And the judgment is based on this fact: God's light came into the world, but people loved the darkness more than the light, for their actions were evil. All who do evil hate the light and refuse to go near it for fear their sins will be exposed. But those who do what is right come to the light so others can see that they are doing what God wants."

It is a very simple requirement to receive and believe in the Son according to Scripture. There is no need for any ritual or something we must accomplish to believe and receive. If it required some task to be acceptable or worthy to receive this gift — it would no longer be a gift.

We don't need complicated, so God provided a gift. God made it simple, so we have no excuses. We either accept His gift, or we reject it. Our reason doesn't matter because what does matter is that we receive His gift and accept our salvation.

Scripture has Explanations Regarding our Skepticism and our Future without Him

Romans 1:21

"Yes, they knew God, but they wouldn't worship him as God or even give him thanks. And they began to think up foolish ideas of what God was like. As a result, their minds became dark and confused."

Romans 1:28

"Since they thought it foolish to acknowledge God, he abandoned them to their foolish thinking and let them do things that should never be done."

1 Corinthians 1:22

"It is foolish to the Jews, who ask for signs from heaven. And it is foolish to the Greeks, who seek human wisdom."

1 Corinthians 1:25

"This foolish plan of God is wiser than the wisest of human plans, and God's weakness is stronger than the greatest of human strength."

1 Corinthians 2:14

"But people who aren't spiritual can't receive these truths from God's Spirit. It all sounds foolish to them and they can't understand it, for only those who are spiritual can understand what the Spirit means."

And just think — it doesn't matter how you became involved in all of this. You can become involved by making choices that will welcome the Lord into your life full-time. It doesn't matter how you got into this situation as long as you know how to get through and experience the Lord's hand throughout. Then, when life here ends, you will be prepared to spend eternity at the location of His choice — Heaven.

Looking to the Lord and accepting His gift of salvation will place you directly in the hands of your Creator and exactly where God wants you to be. You will have accepted His plan for you and will return to Him when your eternity begins. The Bible tells us that Jesus rejoices when a saint comes home to spend eternity with Him. Make Jesus happy, accept His free gift, and get your name added to the Book of Life that He keeps in heaven.

It is the roster you want your name written in because all whose name is written in this book (Lambs Book of Life) will, on Judgment Day, be separated and set apart to spend their eternal life in Heaven. This solution is the perfect end to life on earth with numerous gifts given to the Son by the Father that we inherent because we belong to Christs' family — The Bride.

Don't forget what the Lord tells us about wisdom and some of the great benefits accompanying our obedience to His Truths. God's wisdom is far greater than the accumulated knowledge of man. Our understanding and thinking cannot encompass the things of God as we see in Scripture (Isaiah 55:9).

The Wisdom of God Revealed

Proverbs 3:1-18
"My child, never forget the things I have taught you. Store my commands in your heart. If you do this, you will live many years, and your life will be satisfying."

"Never let loyalty and kindness leave you! Tie them around your neck as a reminder. Write them deep within your heart. Then you will find favor with both God and people, and you will earn a good reputation."

"Trust in the Lord with all your heart; do not depend on your own understanding. <u>Seek his will in all you do, and he will show you which path to take.</u> Don't be impressed with your own wisdom. Instead, fear the Lord and turn away from evil."

"Then you will have healing for your body and strength for your bones. Honor the Lord with your wealth and with the best part of everything you produce. Then he will fill your barns with grain, and your vats will overflow with good wine."

"My child, don't reject the Lord's discipline, and don't be upset when he corrects you. For the Lord corrects those he loves, just as a father corrects a child in whom he delights. Joyful is the person who finds wisdom, the one who gains understanding."

"For wisdom is more profitable than silver, and her wages are better than gold. Wisdom is more precious than rubies; nothing you desire can compare with her."

"She offers you long life in her right hand, and riches and honor in her left. She will guide you down delightful paths; all her ways are satisfying. Wisdom is a tree of life to those who embrace her; happy are those who hold her tightly."

Obedience to His Word is an action on our part that opens up to us a wonderful life, giving us wisdom beyond ourselves that produces a great harvest throughout life. It provides us the spiritual insight we need, builds our trust in Him, increases our faith, yields strength for our body, increases blessings, causes us to be productive, provides the required correction to guide us, and brings satisfaction and great happiness to our lives.

Our becoming involved has tremendous opportunities that are awaiting our attention. Do yourself a favor, latch onto the Lord while there is still time, and replace your questions with godly answers. Travels with the Lord are an adventure in living. Your participation is requested. Choose to yield yourself to His calling and take hold of the

Truths in Scripture that change lives and transform humans to become witnesses for God!

The promises of God are for every believer without respect for your past or present condition. The Lord wants you to choose His Ways and for you to allow Him to bring into your life His Presence and fullness. You are one choice away from starting over and beginning a new life. One that God intended for you to make since you were placed here to become involved in all of this!

Chapter 10

What Does All This Obedience Mean?

This final chapter provides a mind picture, a mental photograph, of the path God would prefer we follow. He gives us glimpses of what's ahead in Bible verses using common references to matters apparent during His time on earth. These references enlighten our understanding and reveal great wisdom in living life — even today!

The references He used were familiar to the people of that day. The connections were given to familiarize the people with a common event that would best explain His point of conversation. Just because some of the references are not common to us today doesn't mean we can no longer learn from His wisdom in parables and apply them to our lives these many years later.

Let me give you an example of what I mean. There are verses in the Bible that once made little sense to me because of what they referenced. For example, the eye of the needle was used in Matthew, as seen below:

Matthew 19:24
"I'll say it again—it is easier for a camel to go through the eye of a needle than for a rich person to enter the Kingdom of God!"

What in the world is he talking about? This subject is also found in Mark 10:25 and Luke 18:25. If we can see how it applied during the time of Christ to explain its visual application and purpose, we can better determine what it means for us today. This phrase adds quite a lot to our understanding, and I will explain.

Back when Jesus walked the earth, walls were many times built around a city for protection. Gates were constructed to allow passage for social and trade activities but were fortified for protection. Passage for their armies needed this size of opening to enter or leave the city. These gates were made to keep out unwanted forces and were carefully guarded to ensure the safety of the cities inhabitants.

Smaller openings were also made in the walls to accommodate individuals' traveling in and out of the city. These openings were designated for people to use only. They were not large enough for livestock and commodities to come through. If such were to enter or depart, they used the larger gates to the city. Either way of passage would provide the necessary space and still provide the city with safety because both were closely guarded.

When we see referenced 'the eye of the needle,' we then understand what the smaller openings were and how they were used, and the reason for their importance. This narrow passage allowed approved people to enter and leave the city and caused no need to open the larger gates. This passage had a specific use and restricted access for something as significant as an army or multiple people to enter at once.

This smaller opening regulated the flow of people and provided additional security just by the restricted size of the portal. Each individual could then be monitored to ensure their intent could be determined before letting them through. Not a bad idea to minimize unwanted personnel to enter without the guards being aware of their passage.

So, as you visualize this opening and its size, you see its intent was to protect those inside the walls. Knowing this, you better understand its purpose. Because of its size, a camel would find it almost impossible to enter the city through this portal (the eye). The narrow opening would not accommodate an adult camel and certainly not with cargo or baggage on its back.

Now, take into consideration a human with baggage or some commodity he was carrying. Could he manage his way through this type of opening? The size was so restrictive it would not accommodate any volume or any large payload. Hence, the eye was a restricted opening used with the specific purpose of safety.

Read the Following Bible verse that References the Narrow Gate

Matthew 7:13-14
"You can enter God's Kingdom only through the narrow gate. The highway to hell is broad, and its gate is wide for the many who choose that way. But the gateway to life is very narrow and the road is difficult, and only a few ever find it."

Scripture tells us the path to the Lord is not selected by everyone. Some approach Heaven but do not rid themselves of sin baggage that is not acceptable for entrance. This thought can be puzzling until you realize the road to the Lord is not nearly as wide as the road to eternal destruction.

God's pathway is chosen, and it is smaller in size and does not accommodate those relying on good works. We must purposely choose to follow the Lord to enter the Narrow Gate! Our passage depends on our choice to accept God's direction and base our choice on Scripture — not man's logic.

Life and our human nature place us in the sin category as determined by Adam and Eve during their stay in the Garden of Eden. They failed God and were blatantly disobedient to His command. Their act of disobedience allowed sin to enter the world and changed all of humanity's lives forever.

The sin they allowed to enter started accumulating baggage that became added weight to their lives. It figuratively became so burdensome they could not maneuver as before and needed relief from their sin burden from that point on. God did not design us to be weighted down by sin and its consequences. The more we continue to accumulate sins cargo (baggage), the more restricted we become.

As it worked out, God made room for a savior to be sent, Jesus, to lighten our load and make life easier to travel. The 'baggage' we accumulate consists of unforgiven sin, shame, fear, sickness, guilt, unforgiveness of others, fleshly desires, revenge, etc. All that baggage that sin brings mounts up and becomes heavier as we move forward in life. It also restricts us from moving through life easily and distracts us from focusing on the Lord and enjoying life to its fullest.

The Bible Regarding Life's Burdens and God's Relief to Comfort Us

Psalm 55:22
"Give your burdens to the Lord, and he will take care of you. He will not permit the godly to slip and fall."

Matthew 11:28
"Then Jesus said, 'Come to me, all of you who are weary and carry heavy burdens, and I will give you rest.'"

Matthew 11:30
"For my yoke is easy to bear, and the burden I give you is light."

So how do we receive a less burdensome life? The light we are given is not only less burdensome, but God's illumination of the entire picture from His point of view brings relief. His light reveals our next best step.

Call upon the Lord to help you identify the problem and repent of those things needing to be forgiven. Pursue a relationship with the Lord and cause yourself to become familiar with God's Word — the

Bible. Seek the principles and guidance God provides for each area needing His help and diligently practice the principles He provides.

The Lord is faithful in fulfilling His promises, and you will soon find this true as you look back on your life since you accepted the Lord. His ways are less burdensome, and the relief from those many burdens life brings will become lighter and lighter as we participate. That means we can be relieved of the excess baggage we accumulate living without Him. Our God seeks what is best for us and carries out His plan as we cooperate and remain obedient to Him.

You will find that less baggage will free you to travel more efficiently, and the Narrow Path to Him will not seem so small. The 'eye of the needle' will become large enough for you to travel in the direction most comfortable, and the heaviness of sin will not need to be carried any further. Learning to lay down our burdensome load is a process that brings many blessings and opportunities that are set before us.

Listen in Your Mind to the Scenario that is Taking Place

Luke 5:1-10:
"One day as Jesus was preaching on the shore of the Sea of Galilee, great crowds pressed in on him to listen to the word of God. He noticed two empty boats at the water's edge, for the fishermen had left them and were washing their nets."

"Stepping into one of the boats, Jesus asked Simon, its owner, to push it out into the water. So he sat in the boat and taught the crowds from there."

"When he had finished speaking, he said to Simon, 'Now go out where it is deeper, and let down your nets to catch some fish.'"

"Master," Simon replied, "we worked hard all last night and didn't catch a thing. But if you say so, I'll let the nets down again."

"And this time their nets were so full of fish they began to tear! A shout for help brought their partners in the other boat, and soon both boats were filled with fish and on the verge of sinking."

"When Simon Peter realized what had happened, he fell to his knees before Jesus and said, 'Oh, Lord, please leave me—I'm such a sinful man.' For he was awestruck by the number of fish they had caught, as were the others with him. His partners, James and John, the sons of Zebedee, were also amazed."

In this particular story, Jesus had started to gather His disciples together. Luke gives an account of how Jesus began the selection process. Consider how Jesus exposed the natural flesh of a person and how distinctly different we see this picture unfold as Peter uses his free will to choose for himself what he wants. Either follow after the Lord's instructions or base his decision on his recent overnight fishing experience.

Peter, James, and John had just spent all night fishing. They were professional fishermen, but after an all-night attempt, they came up empty. After they finished, they cleaned the nets they used to make ready for their next fishing expedition. This net cleaning preparation is standard procedure for those making their livelihood fishing from a boat. Remember, all three were skilled fishermen and had used their natural abilities all night without getting any fish — not even one.

As Jesus completes his sermon to the locals, He turns to Peter and tells him to go back out into the deeper water and cast his nets. What would Jesus know about fishing compared to professional fishermen? Besides, Peter and the boys were very tired from fishing all night and had just washed their nets in readiness for another day. Cleaning a net is also hard work but necessary to ensure their nets would last as long as possible because of the expense of replacing them.

And, Jesus was a preacher, not a professional fisherman like they were, so how would He know better than them? A preacher of the gospel would have subjects he could teach sound biblical principles, but fishing was probably not one of them — fishing for fish, that is. Fishing for men was a whole new concept unknown to them until later.

As Peter heard the Lord speak, his flesh cried out that he was tired, and because he caught nothing fishing all night, it was not even reasonable to go out again. This command was illogical and seemed a complete waste of time considering how he felt and his recent fishing experience.

As he contemplated the Lord's request, he came into direct contact with what everyone comes up against all the time. Our flesh and our logical thinking tell us one thing, and the Spirit of God tells us something entirely different. As Peter evaluated what his flesh was telling him and what the Lord was telling him — he had to choose to follow after his feelings or follow after what the Lord had instructed him.

Peter's first act of obedience was to allow Jesus to use his boat from which to preach His sermon to the crowds. That first act of obedience, on Peter's part, was not that difficult. It didn't require his full participation but only a yes, Lord. The second act of obedience was much more challenging because it called for Peter's full cooperation and denial of his tired, exhausted body and would require him to entirely deny his logical thinking if he were to follow this command from the Lord.

This situation is a common juncture in all our lives, and we each must continually choose between the two. On the one hand, is the flesh crying out to be satisfied and on the other hand, is the Lord instructing us. We must decide which voice to follow. Our response will reflect our choice. This juncture is where we can falter depending on who's voice we choose to entertain. The flesh will momentarily be satisfied if we choose it. The Holy Spirit will be delighted if we decide to follow after his leading and deny our flesh.

To follow after the Spirit of the Lord is called obedience. To follow after our fleshly desire is called disobedience. The choice we make determines our next step in the direction of abundant living. This choice will not be denied, and our selection will be evident by our next move.

There is no way to avoid making a choice. And, as you can see, the choice is left entirely up to us.

As Peter contemplated what his flesh was telling him against what the Lord had instructed him to do, he realized that he had to make a choice. As we can picture from this story, Peter chose to follow after the Lord, and look what happened? What seemed unreasonable in the flesh because of feelings and logical thinking became unimportant based on the results.

Peter's choice to be obedient became obvious and immediate based on his godly choice. As Peter and the boys pulled in a catch that was so large, it almost capsized two boats. Seeing this happening gave all the fishermen a glimpse of why obedience is so rewarding in so many ways.

Peter stepped out in faith, and his obedience cast him one more step into his future. Even though he did not feel like doing it, his one step in faith and obedience placed him directly where the Lord wanted him. Not only did the Lord bless Peter, but the overflow of blessings became evident and beneficial to all those involved.

Everyone was blessed beyond belief and witnessed God at work. In addition, Peter was able to see Jesus more clearly. His encounter with the Lord revealed to him exactly who he was talking to and adjusted his perception of himself in making better decisions.

When we are obedient to God and receive His blessings, don't you think that all those around us will be blessed as well? This principle from making good choices turns the Lord loose in our lives so we can experience a whole new dimension of living. The deeper water that Peter cast his nets into gives us a clue that the Lord wants to take us deeper in our relationship with Him as well.

Peter cast not only his nets into deeper water, but his action of obedience caused him to grow in faith in the Lord because of his new experience. Our obedience gives us another view from a godly perspective into the things of God and what He wants for us! Our God desires to deepen our walk with Him, and numerous occasions will occur right in our presence to draw us to choose obedience to the Lord rather than respond with our worldly thinking and natural tendencies (flesh).

These occurrences are intentional and can be viewed as opportunities the Lord makes available to each believer so we will grow in our trust in Him and allow our faith to be expanded when practiced. We are capable of continual growth in the wisdom of God and are daily challenged to submit ourselves to the knowledge of God for our duration of living on the earth. Our indulgence and submersion into God's Word can yield unlimited catches (blessings) that will fill us to overflowing with much excess to help others.

God doesn't bless us just so we are prosperous only, but to fill us up so we can channel His warehouse of blessings to as many people as possible. Becoming a vessel for the Lord takes on many shapes and areas that broaden our scope of vision and improve our ability to bless others we come into contact with along our journey. Life is more than just about us; it also includes many opportunities to serve others with the many blessings God provides.

If you thought one way then learned later, your wisdom was limited; wouldn't you choose to take the path less complicated and more rewarding? I think we all would prefer the path that places us on the road God has chosen best for us. This choice to take God's selected approach requires our obedience to God's Word whether we feel like it or not. Our feelings and emotions reveal the desires of our flesh, and we must choose the One we are going to follow!

To follow after God, we must deny our fleshly desires and choose to follow His Word. The Bible isn't written to give us a bunch of rules to follow — that's religion. The Bible provides us a map revealing how our choices in life give direction to our path. This written map offers the guidelines to meet our future and choose the consequences we desire. God's Word provides wisdom for our decision-making and gives us the best way to proceed.

If you choose what God biblically instructs you — your future will follow with certain prosperity and fulness of life. Prosperity does not necessarily mean you'll become rich with money. No, that's not just what is being said, but it is a possibility. The wisdom we learn from God surpasses all-natural knowledge and reaches into the treasury of God, where unlimited treasures of excellence reside. Godly morsels of wisdom include knowledge, understanding, power in the Holy Spirit, protection from the evil one, and riches beyond our earthly estimation.

These riches are only attainable as we reach out in obedience to explore the wisdom of God working in our lives. He is ever calling us to Himself so that He can bring the treasures unseen by humankind into reality. We must continually choose to be obedient and adhere to His instructions if we want to see and experience the promises that God has for each believer and what He wants to materialize in our lives.

Even though Peter stumbled through life, he continually sought after the Lord and was continually moving in the right direction. Did God forsake him because he stumbled so much? No, He allowed Peter to travel at his own pace, always being available as Peter grew in wisdom and knowledge of the One who was prompting him. If we continually choose godly principles, we too will obtain the blessings that God intended for each believer.

The Obedience of Jesus

Romans 10:5
*"For Moses writes that the law's way of making a person right with God requires **obedience** to all of its commands."*

As you can see from the above Scripture, the Law gave us the written conditions necessary to have a right standing with God. Fulfilling the Law would have cleared us of sin, but our nature is sinful because of the disobedience committed in the Garden. Always remember, this condition of sin is not tolerable by God.

Our problem is — we cannot obey every commandment written in the Law. This condition we find ourselves in presents quite a dilemma when you consider what we're up against. Our efforts to be saved from the grasp of sin brought into our lives at birth are futile without God. On our own, we find ourselves in an impossible situation with no way out!

But With God Included

Romans 5:19
"For as by one man's disobedience (Adam) many were made sinners, so also by one Man's obedience (Jesus) many will be made righteous."

Adam's disobedience made us all sinners. But, by the obedience of Jesus, we can now fulfill the Law by faith in the Son of God. Why? Because of what He accomplished on the cross by dying in our place.

Scripture Tells why God sent His Son into the World

1 John 3:5
"And you know that Jesus came to take away our sins, and there is no sin in him."

Having no sin, Jesus came into the world and became the perfect sacrifice for our sins that was acceptable to God. Thus, if we accept Him by faith, we too are removed from the curse of sin. Our dilemma of being born into sin is resolved! We trade our sin by faith and believe that Jesus paid the price we owed to God. Another deal we can't beat anywhere else!

So What Did Christ Do?

He was born into the world to become the sinless sacrifice that would be acceptable to God for the forgiveness of sin. His 33-1/2 year journey on earth required Him to follow after numerous Scriptures that referenced the coming Messiah and His purpose.

Philippians 2:8
"He humbled himself in obedience to God and died a criminal's death on a cross."

Hebrews 5:8
"Even though Jesus was God's Son, he learned obedience from the things he suffered."

Jesus Was the Messiah

John 4:25-26
"The woman said, 'I know the Messiah is coming — the one who is called Christ. When he comes, he will explain everything to us.' Then Jesus told her, <u>I Am the Messiah.</u>"

Over 300 biblical verses gave revelation (Bible prophecies of things to come) to His future coming, and His fulfillment of each verse was required. His obedience to the Scriptures had to be fulfilled to the letter for Him to remain the perfect sacrifice for our sin that God would accept.

What Does This Mean?

Scriptures describe in great detail through the prophets regarding the Messiah's life, death, and resurrection. And, Jesus fulfilled each of these prophecies in every detail. So now, there can be no doubt that Jesus Christ was that promised Messiah.

Jesus, the Christ, fulfilled just as was prophesied and completed every task God had set before Him to save the world from sin and damnation. Ultimately, He gave each person born into sin the opportunity to choose salvation and freely fulfill the Law in Christ. And thus obtain salvation through Jesus, the perfect sacrifice, which is obtainable by faith.

The obedience of Jesus, the Son of God, was necessary to fulfill His purpose on earth. The obedience of Jesus became life-saving as a direct result. A life could then be saved from sin and the fatal consequences it brings.

Even the Son of God served His Father by responding in obedience to His every request. His fulfillment of the Scriptures provides us with a clear picture of how our actions should appear if we choose to follow after the Lord. Jesus is the example we should follow after and adhere to His every command if we choose to be led in the direction God desires for every believer.

Consider to Whom You Serve

Romans 6:16

"Know ye not, that to whom ye yield yourselves servants to obey, his servants ye are to whom ye obey; whether of sin unto death, or of obedience unto righteousness?" (KJV)

Our very actions reveal to whom we serve. If we don't serve the Lord, then we are serving ourselves and the ruler of this world, Satan. If we don't choose the Lord and His direction to salvation, then we remain in the hands of the devil. We are then subject to Satan's many divisive ways and his relentless attempts to divert us and keep us away from the knowledge of salvation God offers.

Luke 4:8

Jesus replied, "The Scriptures say, 'You must worship the Lord your God and serve only him.'"

We can have success in life by making biblical choices and becoming a living example of the promises of God in real-time. Doing our part in being obedient to Scripture will cause the Lord to implement His action in making it materialize. He is glorified in our obedience, and He is waiting and wanting us to take Him up on His many promises.

In living our lives following Scripture, we become a witness to the truth of God's Word and are a living example that all can see, touch, feel and relate to. Our obedience to the Lord releases the fullness of God's Word in us and is a clear indicator of the reality of God.

Almost every one of us needs shoulder pads and a helmet to get to the end of life in one piece. But, the Lord already knows that we can rely on Him for our protective gear and only suffer minor injuries. The school of disobedience is always open because if we only function in the natural realm of life, we will never obtain God's best. And remember, the learning curve can be slow if your head is hard like mine.

I certainly have a few lumps and bumps that could have been avoided, but I thought there for a while I was tough enough and could charge my way through life without His help. I did make it downfield, but I could have avoided several 325-pound ball players waiting for me had I chosen to follow after the Lord much sooner.

I'm healed up pretty good now, but I do have a few scars that reveal my playing years alone were not favorable or in my best interest. I had to find out for myself, and the Lord let me. My free will was utilized to a great extent in the wrong direction. Numerous obstacles could have been avoided had I started earlier in life to be obedient.

Since I started making better choices, my path has become much smoother. Why? Because I learned to hear His voice and follow directions as He led me closer to the end zone. I began to follow more closely His instructions and witnessed how they provided a much easier path of resistance.

I'm much closer to the goal line now, and I'm much wiser than earlier in my life. I'm still enjoying being in the game of life and looking forward to the winning final touchdown that awaits me. I want to cross that goal line knowing God better today than I ever have before and enjoy the life He's given me to the fullest. When the game of life is over down here, I can go to my real home and spend Eternity with the Coach who put me in the game many seasons ago.

This life has been fun, and I hope it will be fun for you as well. Since the Lord has forgiven me for all the fumbles, missed opportunities, stubborn will, wrong decisions, fleshly desires, incorrect decisions, not following His guidance, and trying to do it my way and prove to Him I'm capable alone — I'm happy and thankful.

When I was not trusting Him when I should have, and failing to step out in faith and run with the ball instead of just standing there, then I'm good to go because of His saving grace and mercy that saw me through to the end!

He has forgiven me, seen me through anyway, and given me the opportunity to succeed despite my stubborn personality. I'm so full of joy to be a part of the winning team and arrive at the end of life to enter into His Presence. Leaving all this training behind and wanting to see what's ahead is exciting. The winner's circle lies just down field for each of us, and knowing where you're going is such a wonderful ending to life.

I should say beginning. Eternity with the Lord is somewhat described in the Bible, but even the partial view in my mind can bring only excitement to my spirit. I hope to see you there when your life here is over, and you pass through that portal of life into Eternity.

I'll be the happy old man visiting with everyone I can find that I knew down here. I will be congratulating them for their excellent choices on earth and hopefully eating with them at their mansion or mine. I hope to see you there when your journey down here is complete! I'll keep an eye out for you so I can celebrate your arrival.

CPSIA information can be obtained
at www.ICGtesting.com
Printed in the USA
LVHW030041020222
709975LV00001B/7